MIKE O'BRIEN was born in Australia and moved to Europe with his family in the late sixties. After a short-lived career as a singer-songwriter with various record companies, and another even shorter period with a music management company, he co-founded the comedy label Laughing Stock Productions in 1991. He lives in Buckinghamshire with his wife and daughter, has no hobbies, and watches too much television.

BRUCE DESSAU has been the comedy critic for London's *Evening Standard* since 2001. He has written numerous books about British humour. His favourites are his biographies of Reeves and Mortimer, and Rowan Atkinson. He spends far too much time lurking at the back of stand-up clubs with a notebook, laughing a lot, but only occasionally out loud. He went to the same school as Alan Davies and once asked Stephen Mangan from *Green Wing* to autograph a poster of the donkey from *Shrek*.

THE BEST BRITISH STAND-UP AND COMEDY ROUTINES

Edited by Mike O'Brien

CARROLL & GRAF PUBLISHERS
New York

To the memory of Pete Brown: 1954–1993

Carroll & Graf Publishers
An imprint of Avalon Publishing Group, Inc.
245 W. 17th Street
11th Floor
New York NY 10011-5300
www.carrollandgraf.com

AVALON
publishing group incorporated

First published in the UK by Constable,
an imprint of Constable & Robinson Ltd, 2006

First Carroll & Graf edition, 2006

ISBN-13: 978-0-78671-858-0
ISBN-10: 0-7867-1858-7

Printed and bound in the EU

CONTENTS

12: Monty Python's Flying Circus

13: Mark Thomas

People ask me about the secret of comedy. Well, the secret of great comedy is timing. For example, if you the audience come here tonight, and I arrive one week later, that's bad timing ... I've noticed it makes a difference even one day out ...

Arnold Brown

FOREWORD

At the end of 2005, I was contacted at Laughing Stock Productions by book publishers Constable & Robinson wanting to talk to me about doing a book for them based on a set of recordings of stand-up and comedy routines.

Initially, it seemed an odd request. But I knew that Constable & Robinson had published the well-received *Love All the People*, a collection of Bill Hicks' letters, lyrics and comedy transcripts, and when the role of editor of the book was mentioned, I agreed to meet.

The idea was to publish a book of profiles of each of the bestselling comics who had featured on *The Very Best of Laughing Stock*, a CD we had released in the late nineties. The profiles would include interview material, and be accompanied by transcripts of the performances and a copy of the CD itself. A comedy snapshot of the last thirty years in book and audio form.

My enjoyable role was to find a profile writer, obtain copyright consents, select and edit material for transcription, and deliver the book and re-mastered CD in book publishers' time (always six months ahead of normal Earth time).

The greatest pleasure was reading and selecting the transcripts. These performers know how to make an audience laugh, whether in a concert hall or a television studio. But only when you read these manuscripts in the cold light of day, do you become aware of the craft that lies behind the quick-fire routines or the semi-rehearsed set pieces.

And you *will* laugh out loud reading them.

I would like to thank comedy journalist Bruce Dessau and the many artists, artist representatives and copyright owners, such as Amnesty International, Terrence Higgins Trust and Tro Essex Music, for their assistance. And to extend special thanks to commissioning editor Becky Hardie at Constable & Robinson.

Mike O'Brien

INTRODUCTION

What connects the thirteen comedy performers/comedy teams featured here, apart from the fact that they are all stomach-ticklingly, side-splittingly, face-achingly funny? Great minds have wrestled with the question of what makes one person funny, and another as painful as jamming your thumb in the car door. Is it class, religion, upbringing? Were they bullies, or the bullied? Some answers you'll find in these pages, where I've drawn on past interviews and filled in the gaps with new ones. Other answers I couldn't get if I tied my subjects to a table and put thumbscrews on their nipples. (Although between you and me there are a couple of people on this list who might like that.)

Looking at the line-up we have a melting pot, from the upper crust to the positively crusty. Some of the people involved are so posh they make Judith Chalmers seem rough. Others are working class and proud of it. Yet others are American and embarrassed by it.

What you have in your hands is a snapshot of classic comedy from the last thirty years. At least one of the sketches here is so famous it has been spoofed (badly) by a prime minister. Another helped to turn an unknown comedian from the north-east of England into a star almost overnight. Not long after his appearance doing this timeless routine he went from living in a 'shoebox in t'middle of t'road' to living in a rectory in Oxfordshire.

There is politics with a small 'p', and politics with a big 'P'. Lenny Henry in the guise of Delbert Wilkins tackles racism, and the late, great Bill Hicks tackles pornography. There is Eddie Izzard making it up as he goes along, and Arnold Brown caressing every lovingly crafted word. Pete & Dud reflect on the miracle of birth; Jo Brand ponders her Hastings childhood.

But what do they all have in common? Apart from the fact that they all appeared on *The Very Best of Laughing Stock*, the CD released in 1998, I could suggest the link is that I've interviewed almost all of them at pivotal points in their careers. Bill Hicks over the phone, Peter Cook over Bloody Marys. I quizzed Eddie Izzard as he popped into a dress at the Brighton Centre, Michael Palin as he stopped off in London in the middle of another globe-trotting trip.

I met Sean Hughes soon after he became the youngest person ever to win the coveted Perrier Award. I probed Lenny Henry when he had added another string to his ever-burgeoning bow and made a documentary about his love of funk. I prodded Rory Bremner in his office when he had just left the BBC and was working on his first satirical show for Channel 4. And I enticed Rowan Atkinson out of his shell when he had made the move from Blackadder to Bean.

I spoke to Steve Coogan while he did the best acting job of his life – convincing me that *Around the World in 80 Days* was a very good film. I grilled Jo Brand over lunch in Joe Allen's restaurant in Covent Garden. Greg Proops, Mark Thomas and Arnold Brown I interviewed especially for this book. Dudley Moore and Graham Chapman were the only two who got away, by virtue of being dead.

Some have, shall we say, been a bit of a challenge: some I would not want to spend an evening with. But I was interested in all of them because all have produced towering pieces of work that will be talked about for years to come. Comedy is what separates us from the animals. Human beings have made jokes in the worst conditions, even in the concentration camps. It is one of those vital forces that make life worth living.

When I was growing up in the pre-Sky Plus age, people used to run home for Monty Python and its ilk. In fact Steve Coogan recalls how he would call his father in from the garden when *Fawlty Towers* was about to come on. No-one is ever going to run home for *What not to Wear* or *Casualty*. OK, so they might record them on Sky Plus, but you know what I'm getting at. Humour is the very stuff of life. To hear someone say, 'I don't like comedy,' is like hearing someone say, 'I don't like food,' or 'I don't like air.'

Comedy is not a science. You cannot concoct it in a test tube or by computer, though they've tried. And despite the proliferation of comedy courses, you cannot learn it at evening class. It is something that either you grasp or you don't. Jack Dee once told me that comedy is the bastard art. And that sums it up nicely. All the people in this book and on this CD are consummate exponents of the comic art – that is, highly artistic bastards.

Bruce Dessau

ACKNOWLEDGEMENTS

'The Devil', 'Schoolmaster' © Atkinson/Curtis/Goodall
Transcripts courtesy of Amnesty International
'George Bush', 'Henry VIII' 'Hello Hastings' © Jo Brand
Transcripts courtesy of Laughing Stock Productions
'John Major', 'Michael Heseltine', 'Prince Charles', 'The Queen' ©
Langdon/Atkinson/Fortune/Magnusson/Hardie
Transcripts courtesy of Laughing Stock Productions
'The Secret of Comedy', 'Men's Magazines', 'Life Tips' © Arnold
Brown
Transcripts courtesy of Laughing Stock Productions
'Paul Calf', 'Pauline Calf' © Steve Coogan
Transcripts courtesy of Terrence Higgins Trust
'The Psychiatrist', 'A Bit of a Chat' © Peter Cook
Transcripts courtesy of Tro Essex Music
'Delbert Wilkins', 'Trevor Nettleford' © Lenny Henry
Transcripts courtesy of Amnesty International
'What Is Pornography?' from *Bill Hicks: Relentless* and 'Puppet
People' to 'Polls' from *Bill Hicks: Salvation* courtesy of Arizona Bay
Production Company, Inc. © Bill Hicks
'Alibis for Life', 'Religion', 'Nightclubs' © Sean Hughes
Transcripts courtesy of Laughing Stock Productions
'Advertising', 'The Queen', 'Helen of Troy', 'Cats and Dogs' © Ella
Communications
Transcripts courtesy of Ella Communications/Laughing Stock
Productions
'Channel Tunnel', 'English Pubs' © Greg Proops
Transcripts courtesy of Laughing Stock Productions
'The Parrot Sketch', 'The Four Yorkshiremen' © Monty Python
Transcripts courtesy of Amnesty International
'The War on Terror', 'Christians and Drugs', 'Arms and Asylum' ©
Mark Thomas
Transcripts courtesy of Laughing Stock Productions

BIBLIOGRAPHY

Allen, Tony, *Attitude: Wanna Make Something Of It?*, Gothic Image, 2002.

Bennett, Alan, Cook, Peter, Miller, Jonathan and Moore, Dudley, *Beyond The Fringe*, Methuen, 2003.

Booth, Kevin, *Bill Hicks – Agent of Evolution*, HarperCollins, 2005.

Brand, Jo, *A Load of Old Balls*, Simon & Schuster, 1994.

——, *Sorting Out Billy*, Headline Review, 2005.

——, *It's Different For Girls*, Headline Review, 2006.

Bremner, Rory, with Bird, John and Fortune, John, *You Are Here*, Weidenfeld & Nicolson, 2004.

Cook, Peter, and Moore, Dudley, *The Dagenham Dialogues*, Methuen, 2003.

Cook, William, *Ha Bloody Ha: Comedians Talking*, Fourth Estate, 1994.

——, *Tragically I Was An Only Twin: The Complete Peter Cook*, St Martin's Press, 2003.

——, *The Comedy Store*, Little, Brown, 2001.

Dessau, Bruce, *Rowan Atkinson*, Orion, 2000.

——, *Reeves & Mortimer*, Orion, 1998.

Games, Alexander, *Pete & Dud: An Illustrated Biography*, Andre Deutsch, 1999.

Goldman, Albert/Schiller, Lawrence, *Ladies and Gentlemen – Lenny Bruce!!*, W. H. Allen, 1975.

Hicks, Bill, *Love All The People*, Constable & Robinson, 2005.

Hughes, Sean, *Sean's Book*, Pavilion, 1995.

——, *The Grey Area*, Pavilion, 1995.

Lewishon, Mark, *Radio Times Guide to Comedy*, BBC Books, 2003.

Margolis, Jonathan, *Cleese Encounters*, Chapman, Orion, 1998.

McCabe, Bob, *The Pythons, Autobiography*, Orion, 2003.

Milligan, Spike, *The Essential Spike Milligan*, Fourth Estate, 2002.

Perry, George, *The Life of Python*, Pavilion, 1999.

Reeves, Vic, *Me:Moir*, Virgin, 2006.

Thompson, Ben, *Sunshine On Putty*, Fourth Estate, 2004.

Thompson, Harry, *Peter Cook: A Biography*, Hodder & Stoughton, 1997.

True, Cynthia, *American Scream – The Bill Hicks Story*, Sidgwick & Jackson, 2002.

Wilmut, Roger, *From Fringe to Flying Circus*, Book Club Associates, Methuen, 1980.

Wilmut, Roger and Rosengard, Peter, *Didn't You Kill My Mother-in-Law?*, Methuen, 1989.

1. ROWAN ATKINSON

Comedy's missing link

Comedians seem to arrive in ready-made packs. Beyond the Fringe, Monty Python, alternative comedy. It is ironic that, for a profession that invariably champions the solo artist, it is often only when a comedy wave hits the public consciousness en masse that performers become household names. But there are a few exceptions who transcend troupes, defy categorization and provide a bridge between the generations. Among these, Rowan Atkinson is the greatest exception of all.

This unassuming science graduate from north-east England is the ultimate comedy link, hooking together Python's Oxbridge clique and the Comedy Store's radical faction. Having made his name in the late seventies, Atkinson has continued to be a force to be reckoned with, not just on the small screen but in cinemas, where Mr Bean has been a phenomenal success. How many British comedians have truly cracked America since Charlie Chaplin? Peter Sellers, Hugh Grant, maybe Ricky Gervais if we are talking Golden Globes? And Atkinson.

If there was a pivotal year in Atkinson's career it was 1979. He started that year as a cult, and ended it as a star. In the Spring, he had had his own ITV special, *Rowan Atkinson Presents ... Canned Laughter*. In this, the origins of Mr Bean were clearly visible, in the scene where he shaved his entire face, eyebrows too, before gulping down a cup of instant

1

coffee straight from the kettle. In the Autumn, he appeared in BBC2's satirical stab, *Not the Nine O'Clock News*. But it was his live performance at a fundraising event for Amnesty International, 'The Secret Policeman's Ball', which ran at Her Majesty's Theatre in London over four nights in June that year, that put Atkinson firmly on the comedy map.

Atkinson revived a number of his established solo pieces, but his appearance in 'The Four Yorkshiremen' sketch at the Amnesty event clearly illustrates how the Pythons were passing the comedy baton to him. John Cleese was a big champion of Atkinson, having previously seen him at the Hampstead Theatre. When the Amnesty gig was planned, Cleese personally approached Atkinson to appear. And when Eric Idle turned out to be unavailable, Cleese decided that Atkinson was the natural choice to stand in for him in this famous sketch about northern folk reminiscing about their impoverished pasts (for transcript, *see* Monty Python).

If ever there was pressure on a performer it was here. The cause-supporting audience might have been sympathetic, liberal and anti-torture, but when it came to Python anyone who ruined a sketch could expect to be publicly hung, drawn and quartered. Even in these days before DVD everyone knew the words. They had the albums and books, and knew the scripts off by heart as comedy gospels. (I confess, I was one of those annoying playground parrots reciting the lines verbatim.)

In fact the *Not the Nine O'Clock News* team themselves brilliantly laid bare the near-religious fanaticism over Python in a topical skit when the movie *Life of Brian* was accused of blasphemy. In their version the fuss was over '*The General Synod's Life of Christ*', a movie which was said to be taking John Cleese's name in vain – after all, the lead character, Jesus Christ, even had the same initials! And Python was not only worshipped by the Amnesty International audience – it was revered by Atkinson too. As he later told the BBC: 'My defining comic hero at the time was John Cleese.'

Listening again to the Amnesty version of 'The Four Yorkshiremen', one can sense the competitiveness in the voices. Everybody – Cleese, Terry Jones, Michael Palin and Atkinson – wants to top everybody else's laugh. And the new boy does it brilliantly, wringing every atom of humour from his lines, and timing his pauses to laser-guided perfection.

The Amnesty show was the moment when Atkinson was publicly acknowledged as comedy's Next Big Thing. He appeared in three legendary sketches, upstaging the likes of Python, Billy Connolly and Clive James. As well as his 'Yorkshiremen' triumph, he did his famous 'Schoolmaster' sketch, in which he brought the house down simply by reading a class register ('Nibble! Leave Orifice alone'). And he got to play alongside another great hero, Peter Cook, taking the part originally played by Dudley Moore in Beyond the Fringe's enduring 'End of the World' sketch.

Atkinson later summed up the experience of appearing in 'The Four Yorkshiremen' sketch in a BBC *Arena* documentary about the Amnesty galas: 'I was living a fantasy of being on stage with the Python team doing a Monty Python sketch.' He was correct in every respect except for one small detail. Well, quite a big detail actually. 'The Four Yorkshiremen' sketch actually predated Monty Python, having originally been written for the *At Last the 1948 Show*, a forerunner of Python transmitted on ITV in 1967, starring John Cleese and Graham Chapman, alongside bug-eyed Marty Feldman and future Goodie Tim Brooke-Taylor. This was the quartet who wrote the original 'you've-never-had-it-so-good' classic and donned the white dinner jackets to perform it.

The sketch was never actually performed on the television version of *Monty Python's Flying Circus*, but it became associated with Python when they started to perform it live. It was recorded for posterity at their 'Live at Drury Lane' concert in 1974 and appeared again on the *Live at the Hollywood Bowl* compilation.

It is the sign of a truly classic sketch that not even cast changes can diminish it. In fact the cast has undergone some even more radical reconfigurations in recent years as younger comedians weaned on recordings of those early performances paid homage to it. By the summer of 2001, live comedy was bigger than ever and the fortieth anniversary Amnesty gala, entitled 'We Know Where you Live', was held at Wembley Arena. The sketch was done again, with a cast consisting of Eddie Izzard, Harry Enfield, Vic Reeves and Alan Rickman. Izzard in particular was a massive Python fan. Like Atkinson, he can lay claim to the title of honorary Python: he joined the surviving members of the team when they were reunited at the Aspen Comedy Festival in 1998, and appeared in sketches with them during a BBC theme night to mark their thirtieth anniversary in 1999.

By the early eighties, the stars of *Not the Nine O'Clock News* were ready to move on. The BBC had been encouraging Atkinson and his regular writer Richard Curtis to come up with a sitcom. Various ideas were floated. One was a detective variant, pitched as '*Fawlty Towers* meets *Starsky and Hutch*', but it was sensibly felt they should steer clear of any Cleese comparisons. Then one day Atkinson and Curtis were talking about the Hitler Diaries – the bogus papers that had recently hoaxed eminent British expert Sir Hugh Trevor-Roper – and a metaphorical light bulb lit up. What about an alternative version of Britain's past? The rest, as they say, is history. Although only just. The BBC wasn't convinced by the first expensive series set in medieval times and '*The Black Adder*', as the show was initially called, nearly didn't get re-commissioned.

But, by the time the second series of *Blackadder*, set in the court of Elizabeth I, was produced, there had been a number of changes. Most notably Atkinson was now hooking up with a younger post-punk generation of comedians, who were emerging through the ranks via BBC2's *The Young Ones* and Channel 4's groundbreaking early *Comic Strip* films.

4

Significantly, Ben Elton, who had co-written *The Young Ones*, came on board as a writer. Elton's clever use of wordplay and his gift for a no-nonsense gag lent the scripts a new sharpness. Elton was particularly good at coming up with new ways for Blackadder to insult his long-suffering serf Baldrick, played by Tony Robinson: 'Your brain is like the four-headed man-eating haddock fish beast of Aberdeen. It doesn't exist.'

The injection of new blood also included Stephen Fry, who played the wonderfully grovelling courtier Lord Melchett. Meanwhile, the leading light of the new generation of comedians, Rik Mayall, chipped in as thigh-slapping Lord Flashheart. The latter was as dashing as Blackadder was cowardly, and constantly flirtatious ('am I pleased to see you or did I just put a canoe in my pocket?'), turning up to steal Blackadder's bride-to-be. The cameo worked so well that, in the fourth series set in the World War I trenches, Mayall played another Flashheart – this time a flying ace set opposite Baron von Richthofen (played by Mayall's real-life chum Ade Edmondson). Atkinson had cannily married the silliness of Python to the edgier vulgarity of humour's more politically inclined new wave.

Blackadder went from strength to strength during the 1980s, assuming the 'essential viewing' status that Python had once claimed. Other members of the alternative comedy clan joined the fun along the way. Stephen Fry's comedy partner Hugh Laurie was a gloriously chinless Prince Regent in the third series. 'Young One' Nigel Planer also popped up, while Robbie Coltrane really grabbed hold of his role as dictionary-writer Dr Johnson. Atkinson, who had once been the disciple of a previous generation was now giving a master class in comedy to the next generation. When Richard Curtis established Comic Relief in 1985 – a direct fundraising heir to the Amnesty galas and a comedy response to Band Aid – it would be these new comics that he would turn to for support, but Atkinson would be there too, doing special performances of Blackadder and later Mr Bean.

It was the final episode of the fourth series that really made the sitcom cycle special. *Blackadder Goes Forth* painted a picture of modern warfare as bloody, brutal and ultimately pointless, with whole platoons perishing just to gain a few inches of French mud. Captain Blackadder was caught in the middle, between the blimpish General Melchett and the twittish Private Baldrick. Hugh Laurie was on particularly good form as nice but dim public schoolboy Lieutenant George Colthurst St Barleigh (curious fact: there is a race-horse called Strangely Brown who gets his name from the exchange where Blackadder asks George what happened to his fellow Cambridge tiddlywinks players – George replies that Strangely Brown 'copped a packet at Gallipoli').

In the final episode, the horror of war was eloquently conveyed in the nerve-tingling closing scenes, when the platoon have been ordered to go over the top to certain death. Not even the chiselling Blackadder can come up with a cunning plan to get out of this, and as they charge into no-man's-land the picture freezes, they disappear and the screen is filled with a field of poppies.

If Atkinson had carved out a reputation as a comedian with a great gift for verbal humour, he went on to become a comedian with a great gift for visual wit. Mr Bean had been floating around Atkinson's subconscious ever since he had done mimes in revues at Oxford. He had always had the ability to elicit laughs simply by pulling a funny face and now he put that talent to good use with the dialogue-free antics of Bean, a childlike socially inept nerd who could never quite cope with modern life. There were echoes of French comic misfit Jacques Tati, but Bean was something different. Co-writer Richard Curtis described Bean as someone who 'was abandoned at the age of six for being too annoying and had to bring himself up'. Once again Atkinson was going out on a limb. Silent comedy was rarely a success on television but he had the instinctive skill to pull it off.

Bean was an instant success, not just in Britain but around the world. Everyone appreciates a quality pratfall, or getting your hand stuck in a turkey. It was also completely inoffensive family-friendly fun, which made it perfect in-flight entertainment. You could barely get on a plane for a couple of years without being confronted by Mr Bean struggling to park his Mini or change into his trunks on the beach. So much so that in 1997 he made his movie debut in *Bean – The Ultimate Disaster Movie*, which went on to make £140 million at the box office.

Not content with two memorable characters, Atkinson created a third. In Johnny English, he brought the ineptitude of Bean to the special-agent genre. It was not Atkinson's first foray into the world of slapstick spying – in 1983 he had played a bumbling British diplomat in Sean Connery's Bond comeback *Never Say Never Again*. And, of course, Johnny English was not a million miles away from the jet setting undercover operative Atkinson had played in the long-running Barclaycard adverts.

Despite constant calls for the *Blackadder* team to get together again it is unlikely to happen. It is not a case of clashing egos, just a case of clashing schedules. Richard Curtis has Comic Relief and a film career to attend to. Ben Elton seems to spend any spare time he has looking for old rock acts to turn into West End musicals. Stephen Fry has his fingers in more pies than you can shake a stick at. Hugh Laurie is in demand as the unlikeliest American sex symbol this side of Dudley Moore, following his success in medical drama *House*. And Tony Robinson is television's 'Mr History' with *Time Team*. There is always hope though – they reconvened for the last millennium celebrations (maybe if cryogenics or cloning is up to scratch by then they will do it for the next millennium).

As for Rowan Atkinson, he is now working on the second Bean movie, which will apparently feature him creating chaos in the south of France. The project is strictly under wraps, but if you want to see another link between Atkinson and the next generation of modern comedy study the film's production information. The person credited as writer is Simon McBurney, who has directed live shows by French and Saunders, and Lenny Henry, and who appeared as the geeky choirmaster in *The Vicar of Dibley*. He is probably best known in arts circles, however, as the founder of physical stage group Theatre de Complicite. What is less well known about McBurney is that he performed on the opening night of the Comedy Store back in 1979. Legend has it that Atkinson, although established by then, also went down to perform one night, only to go through the wrong door and end up in a strip club by mistake. Which sounds curiously like a storyline for an adult edition of Mr Bean.

Bruce Dessau

'The Devil'

Grand Opera House, Belfast (1980),
Laughing Stock LAFFC 46

Alright, hello. Nice to see you again. Now, as the more perceptive of you probably realize by now, this is Hell, and I am the Devil.

[*Laughter*]

Good evening … You can call me Toby if you like. We try and keep things informal here, as well as infernal. That's just a little joke.

[*Laughter*]

Now you're all here for eternity, which I hardly need tell you is a sod of a long time, [*Laughter*] so you'll get to know everyone pretty well by the end, but for now I'm going to have to split you up into groups.

Are there any questions? Yes?

Um … no, I'm afraid we don't have any toilets. If you'd read your Bible you might have seen that it was damnation *without* relief.

[*Loud laughter*]

So if you didn't go before you came then I'm afraid you're not going to enjoy yourself. [*Laughter*] But then I believe that's the idea.

9

Right, let's split you up then. Can you all hear me still? [*In a louder voice*] Can you hear me at the rack?

[*Laughter*]

Alright. Murderers over here. Thank you. Looters and pillagers over there. Thieves, if you could join them … And bank managers.

[*Loud laughter and applause*]

OK, fornicators, if you could step forward. My God there *are* a lot of you. [*Laughter*] Could I split you up into adulterers and the rest?

Adulterers, if you could just form a line in front of that small guillotine there.

[*Laughter*]

Er … Americans … are you here?

[*Laughter and applause*]

Yes, look, I'm sorry about this. Um, apparently God had some fracas with your founding fathers and damned the entire race in perpetuity. [*Laughter*] He sends particular condolences to the Mormons who He realizes put in a lot of work.

[*Laughter*]

But that's the way the wafer crumbles.

[*Laughter*]

The Iranians I'm afraid can't be with us. Someone's been holding them in purgatory for about nine hundred years.

[*Laughter*]

Sodomites over there … against the wall.

[*Laughter and applause*]

Atheists … atheists over here please. You must be feeling a right bunch of Charlies. [*Laughter*] OK, and Christians. Christians … Ah yes, I'm sorry. I'm afraid the Jews were right …

[*Laughter and applause*]

OK, Moonies, maniacs, Marmite eaters, male models, masochists, mass murders and masseuses, [*Laughter*] if you could just take a pew at the back with the Methodists …

[*Laughter*]

Now, you're the lot who used to kill whales, is that right? Ah yes, I must remember, I've got some strips to tear off you bastards.

Now everyone who saw Monty Python's *Life of Brian* …

[*Laughter*]

Oh yes, I'm afraid He can't take a joke after all.

[*Laughter and applause*]

Alright, now one final thing, we're trying to implement some kind of exchange scheme with the Lord God Almighty, or *Cliff* as you know Him.

[*Laughter*]

Some of you will travel up and have a
decade in heaven, and we're having some
angels down here.

Now, I hardly need tell you that in heaven
you'll be expected to behave in an
exemplary manner, so I hope you do the
exact opposite: tear off their wings, use
their halos for Frisbee practice.

[*Laughter*]

Well, I have to go now unfortunately, but
Beelzebub here will show you the ropes …
and the chains and the electrodes.
[*Laughter*] Um, and I would just like to
leave you with a favourite joke of mine, if
I may, quite apt to the circumstances I
feel, which goes something like, um …

Knock, knock

Who's there?

Death.

Death wh— ?

[*Laughter and applause*]

'Schoolmaster'

'The Secret Policeman's Ball' (Amnesty gala),
Her Majesty's Theatre, London (1979),
Laughing Stock LAFFC 46

Right, quiet please …

[*Laughter*]

Ainslie?

[*Laughter*]

Babcock?

Bland?

Carthorse?

Dint?

Elseworth-Beast-Major?

[*Laughter*]

Elseworth-Beast-Minor?

[*Laughter*]

Fiat?

German?

Haemoglobin?

[*Laughter*]

Have-a-Nut?

[*Laughter*]

Jones M?

Jones N?

Junta?

[*Laughter*]

Loudhailer?

[*Laughter*]

Mattock?

Nancy-Boy-Potter?

Nibble?

[*Laughter*]

Come on, settle down …

Orifice?

[*Laughter*]

Plectrum?

Poins?

Sediment?

[*Laughter*]

Soda?

Taa? … Taa

Under-Manager?

Wicket?

Williams-Wicket?

Williams-Wycherley?

Wycherley-Wicket?

Wycherley-Williams-Wocket?

Zob?

[*Laughter*].

Absent … [*Marks the register*]

Alright, your essays … 'Discuss the contention that Cleopatra had the body of a roll-top desk and the mind of a duck.'

[*Laughter and applause*]

Oxford and Cambridge Board, O-level paper, 1976.

Don't fidget Bland. The answer … Yes.

Jones M, Orifice, Sediment and Under-Manager, see me afterwards.

[*Laughter*]

Most of you of course didn't write nearly enough. Dint, your answer was unreadable.

Put it away, Plectrum …

[*Laughter*]

If I see it once more this period Plectrum I shall have to tweak you. Do you have a solicitor?

[*Laughter*]

You're lying, Plectrum, so I shall tweak you anyway. See me afterwards to be tweaked. Yes, isn't life tragic?

Don't sulk, boy, for God's sake. Has matron seen those boils?

[*Laughter*]

Bland, German, Nancy-Boy-Potter, Under-Manager, Cribbing.

Under-Manager's answer, upside down.

Do you do it deliberately, Under-Manager?
You're a moron, Under-Manager. What are
you? A carbuncle on the backside of
humanity.

[*Laughter*]

Don't snigger, Babcock. It's not funny.
Anthony and Cleopatra is not a funny play.
If Shakespeare had meant it to be funny, he
would have put a joke in it.

[*Laughter and applause*]

There is no joke in *Anthony and Cleopatra*.
You'd know that if you had read it,
wouldn't you, Babcock?

What play of Shakespeare's does have a joke
in it?

Anyone?

The Comedy of Errors, for God's sake! *The
Comedy of Errors* has the joke of two people
looking like each other ... twice.

[*Laughter*]

It's not that funny, German. [*Laughter*] And
the other Shakespearian joke is ...

Nibble! [*Shouting*]

Nibble! Leave Orifice alone!

[*Laughter and applause*]

Right, for the rest of this period you will
write about Enobarbus.

16

Under-Manager, just try and write.

Usual conditions: no conferring, no eating, no cheating, no looking out of the windows, no slang, no slide rules. Use ink only … via a nib if possible.

[*Laughter and applause*]

You may use dividers, but not on each other.

Junta, you're in charge.

[*Laughter and loud applause*]

2. JO BRAND

You don't *have* to be a fully qualified psychiatric nurse ...

Every comedian has to start somewhere, and for Jo Brand it was a Greenpeace benefit in Soho's Wardour Street in 1986. She was 29 and working as a psychiatric nurse. It was a short set at the end of a long evening, based around stories about Freud and one-liners about penis envy. The best thing about having a penis, she mused, was that you could have a piss at the bus stop on the way home from the pub. As they say in the trade, she stormed it, and never looked back.

Or to be more precise, she died on her arse, as they say in the trade. The crowd was drunk, she was drunker, and a heckler shouted, 'You fat cow,' throughout her ordeal. Of course, Brand was upset by the response, but she is made of strong stuff and didn't knock the idea of being a stand-up on the head. She took a break, regrouped her mental forces, wrote more gags, and a few months later started again. And since then she has never looked back.

Brand's defiant early gigs in the face of audience abuse prepared her for a professional career during which she has faced the same treatment from some areas of the media. They have followed the fiendishly logical thought process that if she is fat she must be a feminist, if she is a feminist she must hate men, and if she hates men she must be a lesbian. Maybe the line, 'Never trust a man with testicles,' had something to do with it. And her revision of the traditional notion that the way to a man's heart is through his stomach: 'No. It's through his hankie pocket with a bread knife.' She certainly gets mileage out of the battle of the sexes. 'Men are fantastic. As a concept.' When she got married, she was asked if she was going to take her husband's name. Her response was to shrug her shoulders and ask why would she want to call herself 'Bernard'?

Then again, she is a comedian, these are all jokes, and she tells them very well. Since picking up a Perrier Award nomination in 1992, Brand has been the pre-eminent post-alternative female comedian. She has been so important she has even influenced comedians that started before her. Jenny Eclair had been on the circuit since the early eighties, but when Brand came along it got Eclair's competitive juices flowing. She sorted her act out and went one better than Brand, becoming the first female stand-up to win the Perrier Award in 1995. In 2005, Laura Solon became only the second woman to win it in 25 years.

It is astonishing that, in this era of supposed sexual equality, women have been so marginalized in the world of comedy. The relative paucity of female comedians has vexed theorists since stand-up began. A glance at *Time Out*'s comedy listings suggests that there are around ten male comics to every female.

Being a woman in comedy is a double-edged sword. As Brand has noted, when she was starting out, there were so few women in the business her gender could be a selling point and give her an advantage. It is true that women may find it easier to get gigs because promoters like to have variety on the bill. But whether being patronized in this way is helpful is another question. It essentially means that being a woman in stand-up gets you bracketed with such variety acts as jugglers and magicians (with no offence intended to jugglers and magicians).

This can have more disadvantages further up the career ladder. Television is always keen to snap up new talent and a woman will often attract more attention than a man just because of her novelty value. The result of this is that whereas men might have years to hone their skills before being exposed in people's homes, women might have months. Shazia Mirza, for instance, quickly caused a flurry when she became known as the only female Muslim stand-up. She had barely started her career when 9/11 happened, and she was subsequently approached to appear on *Have I Got News for You*? It was an offer that was too good to be true, but the result was that she had to fight publicly for every laugh in the company of more experienced – male – performers.

In fact, *Have I Got News for You*? is a microcosm of the comedy world. It is very much a boys' club, with a lot of testosterone flying about. Every man wants to get the last laugh. When women are interested in being the witty one, it can have broader drawbacks too. Dawn French recently told me that when she was a teenager she liked to be the funny one in the pub, and while that made her very popular as a friend, boys were less inclined to ask her out – women find funny men sexy, but men want to be top dog in the banter stakes and are less keen on dating funny women.

Comedy may not seem a traditionally 'feminine' profession. What woman in her right mind would want to earn a living slogging up and down the motorways and living on a diet of chips? Jo Brand for a start. And the hours were attractive too. Instead of twelve-hour shifts at the Maudsley Psychiatric Hospital in south London, she worked for an hour and could stay in bed all morning. Comedy was the answer for this scalpel-sharp woman, who was born in 1956 and grew up in Hastings. Judging by the bilious remarks about her hometown in the routine featured here she has no plans to retire there.

Brand was a genuine pioneer. She was certainly not the first female comedian. There had been French and Saunders, Marti Caine, Victoria Wood, and others going back to Joyce Grenfell and beyond to music hall. In the early alternative comedy days there were also Jenny Lecoat and Pauline Melville. But, while many of these comedians were performing to experienced audiences, Brand ventured out on a nightly basis to the new comedy clubs that were opening up. To earn a living, she was performing to audiences unused to live comedy and potentially hostile. Heckles were a way of life. While, 'Get your tits out,' was the usual, Pavlovian put-down for women, Brand was once greeted with, 'Put your tits away.' But, when you've worked the night shift at the Maudsley Hospital, nothing you experience on stage is going to be more frightening. You don't *have* to be a fully qualified psychiatric nurse to work in comedy … but it probably helps.

Having taken up stand-up in her relatively sensible late twenties, her Dr Martens stayed firmly on the ground when the offers started coming in. It is interesting to note that while comedy is ubiquitously compared to rock and roll, some of this country's finest comedians didn't really break through until their first flush of youth was a distant memory. Reeves and Mortimer, and Frank Skinner, were in their thirties before they had a sniff of success, and comedy geriatric Ricky Gervais was pushing forty when he started filming *The Office*. It seems to help if you have had a real life – while comedians may want desperately to escape their experience, it does give them something to talk about on stage.

After a couple of years, Brand was offered a slot on Channel 4's prestigious stand-up showcase, *Friday Night Live*, working under the soubriquet of 'The Sea Monster'. It was only at this point that she gave up her day job. It wasn't simply that she didn't need the money. It was also because she thought there might be a conflict of interest. She lived in dread of a patient coming into the hospital, shouting that they had seen her on television, and being diagnosed as delusional, when all they'd been doing was watching a show.

In 1993, she had her first series on Channel 4, *Through the Cakehole*. While her live act had to be a little diluted for the small screen, her agenda remained essentially the same: men rubbish, trifles brilliant. But clearly aware that 45 minutes about lazy boyfriends and doughnuts might wear a bit thin, she broke up the stand-up routines with sketches, most notably the running gag featuring 'Drudge Squad', a group of exhausted, shopping bag-wielding cops-cum-housewives, who had to balance fighting crime with daily chores.

By the mid-nineties, Brand had become a focused performer, determined to concentrate on a stand-up career. This was an era when you couldn't turn on the television without seeing stand-ups having a bash at sitcoms – everyone, from Ardal O'Hanlon, to Alan Davies, to Dylan Moran, seemed to be at it. Brand shrewdly steered clear of this digression. The difference between stand-up and sitcom isn't just one of process: as a stand-up you also have far more control over your material. However good an actor you are, if you are landed with a duff script there's not a lot you can do about it. There's a saying in the business: 'You can't polish a turd.'

She also recognized her limitations. Even broad sketches were a stretch. By her own admission Brand is no female Brando. In fact, when *Prime Suspect* creator Lynda La Plante (French for 'Linda the Plant', according to the comedian) was writing a murder story set in the world of stand-up, she interviewed Brand while doing her research, and eventually decided to set a scene in a club at which Jo Brand was doing a gig. Brand auditioned for the part of Jo Brand and failed to get it, which gives you some idea of her acting ability.

Yet as a stand-up she was getting better all the time. She was much more subtle than her 'cakes-men-cakes' patter suggested. Brand is not an overtly political comedian, but she smartly smuggled politics into her act by feigning girly indifference to world affairs: 'Civil war in Yugoslavia? That's not going to get the washing up done or the beds made.' Back in the apartheid days, her support for the boycott of South African products was apparently purely accidental: 'I don't buy South African fruit. I don't buy any fucking fruit at all to be honest with you. No chocolate in it, no point.'

As she reached middle age, she became less rigid as to what sort of programmes she would appear in. This worked in her favour, revealing other sides to what had been perceived in some quarters as a one-dimensional character. She managed to transform her bolshy live persona into an intelligent television-friendly personality, doing everything from presenting clip shows celebrating bad ads to the inevitable reality-TV stint. Her double act on *Celebrity Fame Academy* with Ruby Wax, in which she wore a voluminous pair of pants, may well end up being the moment they show on her television obituary.

Brand also took part in a *What Not to Wear* special, in which Trinny and Susannah gave her image an overhaul. The change didn't seem to have a lasting effect. When I saw her on stage six months later, she was still wearing a tent-like black blouse, functional trousers and chunky shoes. She did explain that their supportive bra advice had been very useful though. Apparently, the reinforced scaffolding she now wears means she no longer blinds fourteen-year-old boys – instead she blinds fully grown men. Her frontage is a subject that has inspired many gags over the years: 'Triumph has the bra for the way you are? Isambard Kingdom Brunel has the bra for the way I am.'

She is resolutely unapologetic about her physical size. As she remarked at a gig in Bristol in 1993, 'I thought about trying to lose weight when I was 19 … stone (curious fact: ever the 'eco-conscious' performer, Brand is clearly a believer in recycling her best lines, as evidenced by a routine recorded two years later – 'I got out of Hastings when I was 17 … stone'). She has joked that she once had her jaw wired, but found it hard to force Mr Kipling's Raspberry Fancies through the wire mesh. Apparently, Weightwatchers was never a serious option: 'If you've put on any weight they stab you and throw cottage cheese at you – I went to the newsagents and had a Twix and a much nicer afternoon.'

Since turning forty and becoming more domesticated, Brand has not mellowed in terms of her humour, but has simply found new things to crack gags about. After getting married, she had two children in quick succession. When she was trying to sell her house, the estate agent said it smelt of piss. 'Nothing new there, then,' she reflected, speculating that it might have had something to do with the fact that she had urinated in his briefcase.

Motherhood did mean less time on the road and more time at home, where she started doing more writing. Back in the nineties she had penned *A Load of Old Balls* (Simon & Schuster), which mocked men in history, and on the back page featured a picture of Brand playing up to her image and suggestively cracking a testicle-sized walnut. According to this book, 'Gandhi started a neighbourhood vegetarian club which was a bit like Neighbourhood Watch except you had to grass people up if you spotted them with a sausage.' Meanwhile, Genghis Khan, it claimed, did do some good for Asia Minor: 'Say what you like about Genghis Khan, but when he was around old ladies could walk the streets of Mongolia at night and people could leave their doors unlocked when they went out.' Brand nailed her militant political colours to the mast by including Margaret Thatcher: 'I know she's not a man but I still think she should be strung up by the bollocks.'

Her first novel, *Sorting Out Billy* (Review), suggested that, a decade on, her opinion of men hadn't changed that much. It was about a group of women who, as the title suggests, exact their revenge on a man who has done them wrong. If that storyline echoed Brand's onstage philosophy, her more ambitious second novel drew more directly on her offstage past. *It's Different for Girls* (Headline) was a rites-of-passage tale set in a seaside town and homing in on dysfunctional families and sex, two topics close to the heart of most stand-ups. It demonstrated that Brand is a very skilful writer. When some stand-ups turn novelists, you are aware of the cogs working and the way they are trying to crowbar their set into the narrative. With Brand, however, there is a sense of flow: she created a page-turner.

While the books have been a welcome departure, it is live where the biggest challenge remains. Jo Brand is about the enter uncharted territory. Stand-up is regarded as a young man's game. Brand is neither young or a man, but she intends to keep on performing. Apart from anything else, she will probably enjoy defying the misogynistic critics who have always wanted to write her off. The trouble is fitting it in between parenting, novels and being a well-paid fixture on television. But she's done the hard bit: getting started, and defeating the doubters and the hecklers. Nothing is ever going to be as hard as that first gig. She is not about to cash in her chips – she is more likely to eat them.

Bruce Dessau

'George Bush'

Civic Hall, Aylesbury (2000),
Laughing Stock LAFFCD 0116

Now, I hope you've all been following the American elections, have you? [*Laughter*] 'Cos I think about three million Americans spoilt their ballot papers voting for George W. Bush.

Thank you, the George W. Bush haters at the back. No need to ask what the 'W' stands for, I suppose …

Would have been a good idea if they'd sent some observers from Rwanda or Somalia over to America to sort of supervise the elections in a grown-up way.

[*Laughter*]

'Cos I think, you know, in a democracy voting is incredibly important. It is, and everyone should do it, and that is why I used to ring up every week and try and get Craig out of that fucking Big Brother house.

[*Laughter*]

But the weird thing is, it is actually … It seems to me it's very easy to become a celebrity very quickly these days. You're not a proper celebrity, right, unless you have your own stalker. No, you're not. And a few years ago, when I did my first telly

series, I started getting these very weird
letters from this bloke, in Colchester …

[*Laughter*]

Yes. That was enough to put anyone off,
really … They were quite … They started off
quite nice and then they got kind of a bit
more pervy, and a bit more pervy and then
he sent me a photo of himself and he looked
quite like my dad, which really did my head
in.

[*Laughter*]

And then, I kid you not, about a week after
I got the photo, I was watching a programme
on telly about stalkers, and this bloke was
on it.

[*Laughter*]

He was. Stalking some poor woman in
Colchester … Fucking bastard. Left me for
someone else. I couldn't believe it …

[*Laughter*]

Do you all watch *Who Wants to be a
Millionaire*? Afraid so. Do you think it's a
bit boring? Yes. They're doing their own
version on Channel 5 quite soon called
Fancy a Fuck for a Fiver.

[*Laughter*]

Which I think could be a lot better. I love
Channel 5. It's so tasteful, isn't it?
[*Laughs*] I do like you. You're a great
audience because I'm making comments and
you're all sort of going, 'Yes, quite

right. Yes, I, I think you'll find you're
right on that one.'

[*Laughter*]

'Cos I have to say, you know, I don't know
what you think about people's lives that do
telly and whether you think we sort of kind
of spend our lives snorting cocaine off 14-
year-old boys' arses …

[*Laughter*]

'Cos we do. And that's the only reason I do
it, really.

But people treat us quite weirdly as well,
you know. I was going up to Scotland a few
months ago and I was just like queuing up
to get on the plane and this stewardess
says to me, 'Ooh, there's three of you on
this flight.'

Three what? Three people over the weight
allowance?

[*Laughter*]

Three sad old fuckers that look like opera
singers with a mental illness? What?

And she said, she said, 'No. Shall I tell
you who the other two are?' And I went,
'Yes, please do,' and she said, 'Millicent
Martin, and Madge from *Neighbours*'.

[*Laughter*]

'Now,' she said to me, 'would you like me
to sit you with them?'

Like I've got anything to say to Madge from *Neighbours*, [*Laughter*] apart from your hair's shit and your make-up's worse …

Now, the other thing that a lot of celebrity people are doing recently is coming clean about their drug use. So, I thought why be any different, let me just tell you what I've had. I've had cocaine (obviously), ecstasy, LSD, crack, cannabis and amphetamines …

Well, you get a bit bored waiting for the show to start, you know.

[*Laughter*]

You've got to do your best. And, in fact, last night I had seven Es which is a shit hand at Scrabble and I lost.

[*Laughter*]

Now, I don't know whether you've been led to believe by some hideous tabloids that I don't like men.

[*Laughter*]

Who went 'hear, hear'? Was that a bloke or a woman? Go on, you can tell me. I'm not going to jump off the stage and sit on your face. Let's face it, when I go back and take a run-up the whole fucking lot of you are taken out in one go, aren't you?

[*Laughter*]

So we won't risk that. Who said, 'Hear, hear, men are fantastic'? You're not going to tell me, are you? You're too frightened.

I won't do anything, I promise. I'm quite
nice really …

No, 'cos I mean, I *do* take the piss out of
blokes. Oh, big deal. Can they not take it,
you know? And that's because I do actually
believe that women have the right to be
equal with men and to get the same money as
men get for jobs and things like that. You
know, I think that's fair enough. I do
really …

[*Laughter*]

Was that a 'hear, hear', or a 'ho, ho'?

Obviously, some, some miserable old fucker
that's been dragged out by their missus
tonight. 'Have I got to sit through that
fat lesbo's act again?'

[*Laughter*]

'Can't we go and see Bernard Manning?'

[*Laughter*]

Let's face it, not much to choose between
us, is there, really, in the looks
department.

Poor old Bernard. He's going to die soon.

Hoorah.

[*Laughter*]

And I always think to myself what would it
be like if, if women had male genitalia?
Well, we wouldn't put up with that for a
kick-off, would we? [*Clutches an imaginary
scrotum*]

[*Laughter*]

We'd take one look at the old testicles and we'd be straight down to Boots for some anti-wrinkle cream double quick, wouldn't we?

[*Laughter*]

I'm not going out with them looking like that, thank you. And we'd also probably make some nice little Laura Ashley type holders for them, wouldn't we, in sewing class, so they looked presentable. 'Cos they don't look presentable, men.

And please never feel you have to get them out for our entertainment, because it's a huge mistake or a small mistake, obviously, in a lot of cases.

[*Laughter*]

Some women, I must admit, do have a bit of a jaded view of men and it's caused by something that's happened in their past. And I have to admit to this myself a little bit, because when I was 15 years old I was involved in this rather weird incident with a bloke which to some extent sort of affected my views I suppose.

'Cos I was actually away from home for the first time ever, 15 years old, doing some voluntary work, down the pub in the evenings, getting very drunk indeed and trying to pick up blokes, which is great fun when you're 15, isn't it?

But the trouble is if you're a teenager and you drink alcohol, it makes you do things you wouldn't normally do, doesn't it? Like trampolining in my case …

[*Laughter*]

You see, the thing is once you start drinking and chatting up a member of the opposite sex, misunderstandings arise, don't they? Sometimes women, like young women, kind of feel pressured into sex and you shouldn't do.

You don't have to. There's lots of different ways of doing it. I mean, a guy I went out with when I was a teenager — we used to practice mutual masturbation …

Me in my house. Him in his, you know.

[*Laughter*]

It was, [*Laughs*] much more fun …

'Henry VIII'

From *A Load of Old Balls*,
recorded at Soundbyte Studios, London (1995),
Laughing Stock LAFFC 40

Henry VIII. Henry VIII, or King Syphilis gut-bucket, wife-murderer VIII, as I prefer to call him, was born in 1491, and despite all the paintings we know and love of him looking like a great big beached whale, he was quite athletic as a young man.

At the age of 18, his brother, Arthur, died, and Henry married his widow, Catherine of Aragon. Henry was always an ambitious young man and he thought it best to get the male heir business out of the way before he set off on conquering expeditions. There must have been something dodgy as far as the royal sperm was concerned, because it took bloody ages. Henry always had a bit of an inferiority complex, being the second son, and he grew up to be an egotistical, self-righteous, cruel man; in fact, the last sort of person who should have been King. I often wonder when I read English history why so many of the Royals were such vicious bastards, and I think it's probably because they could be. Give our Queen half a chance and she'd be up the mall with a crossbow, picking off Japanese tourists and nicking their cameras.

Catherine of Aragon had five children but only one of them survived, and unfortunately, as far as Henry was concerned, that one was useless. Mentally handicapped, physically disabled — well, in Tudor-think, both. She was a girl. They were together, Henry and Catherine, that is, for nearly 20 years, but when Catherine began to get hot flushes and started doing a bit of shoplifting, Henry realized she would not be able to have any more children and, like a dutiful, loving husband, he told Catherine not to worry and that everything would be all right.

Did he? Did he Fuck!

He did his utmost to get rid of her without actually bumping her off. Because Henry already had to get a special dispensation from the Pope to marry Catherine, it didn't look good for another favour from the Catholic Church. In fact, as far as the Pope was concerned, he had as much chance of getting a divorce as he did of winning a Gary Lineker look-alike contest, so Henry decided, rather than muck about going through the legal channels of the Catholic Church, he might as well dump them all together and start his own little church. So he became Head of the Church of England. Nice work if you can get it.

At this point he was having a good old flirt with Anne Boleyn who would not give in to his advances unless he agreed to marry her. He did, got her up the duff, and they married secretly. By this time Henry was pretty portly so it was difficult for him to do anything secretly. Unfortunately, Anne Boleyn did not have a son either. Oh drat, she must have thought as the future Elizabeth I popped out. But Henry by this stage started to go a bit bonkers. He must have thought to himself, well, I'm head of the Church of England; I can do what I like now. He found some poor bloke who worked in the Court, accused him of having an affair with Anne Boleyn, tortured him until he said yes, and then had her executed. A bit over the top! I mean, he could have just asked her to move out. In fact, Henry got rid of anyone in his way.

He was a sort of fat, royal combine harvester. Once he was head of the church, he nicked all their money, destroyed many monasteries and anyone who got in the way was disembowelled.

After Anne Boleyn, Henry moved on to Jane Seymour who was said to be homely and sweet. She managed to squeeze a boy child out of her womb, for which she must have gone down on her knees and thanked God for allowing her to continue wearing a nice selection of hats. Unfortunately, and I suppose this is the way life goes, she died 12 days later. Henry then moved on to Anne of Cleves, whom he charmingly named the Flemish Mare. Pity she didn't kick him in the Hampton courts! Their marriage was never consummated. She was lucky! They divorced. He then moved on to Katherine

Howard, who was described by one book I read as a spirited minx — more a reflection on the writer than Katherine Howard, I would have thought. She was accused of adultery and had her head chopped off as well. Finally, Henry finished up with Katherine Parr who is described as amicable. In men's speak, that means nice but ugly. But judging by Henry's record up to this point, it seemed safer to be not that great looking. At least you got to hang onto your head!

Henry didn't execute only women and church people; he did for anyone who got on his nerves. Several of his advisers who annoyed him were destined never to wear glasses again. Henry was an irritable, spiteful, greedy, boorish, sulky little boy of a man. In fact, the only good thing I can think of to say about him was that he was quite easy to find in the maze at Hampton Court on a hot day, because he whiffed so badly.

Legend has it that after Henry died, his body was brought back to London and it was so riddled with disease that it exploded. This has since been known, as he was a big man, as a 21-gut salute …

'Hello Hastings'

Hastings (1995),
Laughing Stock LAFFC 45

BRAND

Hello … Hello, Hastings.

[*Laughter*]

Fantastic to be back. It is. What was that?
That was a little heckle, wasn't it, very
early on? Go on then …

HECKLER

Give him his clothes back!

BRAND

Give him his clothes back? What? Give who
his clothes back? [*Heckler's reference to
Brand's support act Jeff Green, who also
wears all black on stage*]

Oh, you mean my clothes, do you, you sad
old tart? What have you got on then? White
high heels and a curly perm, is that it?

[*Laughter*]

Nice welcome back to Hastings … Thanks very
much, matey. That's very kind indeed. And I
got out of Hastings actually when I was 17
… stone.

[*Laughter*]

Not enough fucking cake shops for me …

I was looking in the encyclopaedia, because
I haven't been, like, back here for ages,
you know, to see if anything had changed
and apparently Hastings' now been twinned
with Bernard Manning's arsehole, so that's
nice, isn't it?

[*Laughter*]

That's not very fair. There are worse
places than Hastings, aren't there? Beirut
and Sarajevo spring to mind …

[*Laughter*]

Do you … do you all consider yourselves to
be grown-ups? No? Because I often wonder,
when did that time come when you think, hmm
… I'm a bit of a grown-up now. And I used
to think it was when I got a mortgage five
years ago, but it's not, is it? It's two
years later on when you're sitting chatting
— because I got a mortgage with a friend —
you're sitting chatting and you say, 'I
know what. Let's borrow a bit of extra
money from the building society, do up the
kitchen.'

That's very grown up, isn't it? So we
borrowed an extra five grand off the
building society, spent it all on sweets …

[*Laughter*]

Because, you know, we all worry about
getting old, because we don't treat old
people very well in this country and I
think we all think, you know, we're going
to be rejected by our relatives and

friends, end up in an old people's home stuck in front of the telly all day with a nurse coming past three times a day and shoving food in our gobs.

Sounds brilliant, doesn't it?

Don't even have to go the toilet, do you? Just piss yourself and they come and sort you out. Do you know what I mean?

[*Laughter*]

What could be better than that?

Because, you know, my dad's getting to be a bit of an old git actually. He … he's getting quite old and he's … he's had a bad year. He's not been very well this year and he's actually been living in a caravan sort just along the coast at Petts Level and, you know … Well, I've made a bit of money out of the telly. I could afford to buy him a house … but he wouldn't let me go out when I was 15 …, so fuck him! Let the old bastard rot down there. That's what I say.

[*Laughter*]

Fuck, all me relatives are in. This is a nightmare … No, because he was so cruel to me when I was a teenager in Hastings, trying to have a good time. Do you know what I mean?

Because, like, when I was 13, I wanted to go out to the disco with me mates, you know, and I wasn't allowed to wear tights. I wasn't allowed to wear makeup. And all my friends would be getting ready to go out looking like Joan Collins. I'd be tagging along behind looking like fucking Keith Chegwin, you know? It was a nightmare.

[*Laughter*]

And it got worse because he did eventually let me out when I was 16, but he'd say to me, 'Be in at eleven or I'll fucking kill you,' right? And I remember one night I came in at ten past eleven, right, and he's sitting there waiting for me. I was terrified. And he got hold of my handbag and he tipped all the contents out on the floor to try and get a clue about where I'd been, and found my contraceptive pills. Oh, god, he went fucking mad, threw a party, couldn't believe I'd got a shag …

[*Laughter*]

And, you know, I was at an all girls' school and everyone in my class was totally ignorant like I was, you know? And I remember one girl actually started her period in geography when we were about 12, which was great, because it stopped us talking about ox-bow lakes for five minutes.

[*Laughter*]

And she put her hand up and went [*Crying noise*], like that. And the teacher said, 'What's the matter with you? She said, I've got a headache and a tummy ache. And the teacher said, I know the problem. You've become a woman …'

[*Laughter*]

And she got one of those sanitary towels out of the drawer that looks like a sleeping bag with loops on the end of it, you know?

[*Laughter*]

Very subtle. And she said to this girl, 'Go on, off you pop and go and sort yourself out. Come back in, in five minutes.' So the girl came back in five minutes later, right, with it *over her head* ...

[*Laughter*]

Loops under her ears because she thought it would make her headache better ...

3. RORY BREMNER

Is it Dawson or Prescott?

The tabloids have a phrase for it: 'reverse ferret'. Compare and contrast the Rory Bremner of today with the Rory Bremner who first appeared on our television screens in the early eighties. The phrase dates from the days when the *Sun*'s editor Kelvin McKenzie used to talk about his journalists sticking a ferret up people's trouser legs when he wanted to wind them up. If, however, McKenzie decided he wanted the same people on his side he'd opt for the alternative withdrawal-of-fangs policy, dubbed the 'reverse ferret'.

More exactly, you could say that Rory Bremner has executed a brilliant reverse ferret in reverse – he started his career cosying up to his viewers by doing nice-but-toothless cricket commentator impersonations and now he is hell-bent on driving a stake into the heart of the establishment with his piercing satire. Back in the early eighties, Bremner was anointed 'the new Mike Yarwood' and had his own BBC show. Now he is ensconced on Channel 4 and it is not for nothing he has been dubbed this government's 'natural opposition'.

Incidentally, at the time of writing, when I say 'this government' I am referring to a Labour government, though with crisis after crisis besetting it, Bremner had better be honing his David Cameron impression if he knows what side his bread is buttered. Actually, he already knows what side his bread is buttered. I saw him on stage in Brighton a month after Cameron became Tory leader and he had already nailed his twenty-first century new-broom sensibility, calling him 'shiny as an iPod'. To borrow from the gospel according to St David, Bremner might have started out as an analogue comedian, but he has worked harder than most to go digital.

Looking back now, Bremner was never really cut out for light entertainment. He is far too much of a comedy heavy-weight. He simply fell into it because there was no other role model for a talented impressionist with a penchant for doing prime ministers. Peter Cook may have done an effective Harold Macmillan, and his early sixties cohort John Bird – more of him later – did a very effective Harold Wilson, but by the late seventies the ability to impersonate somebody else usually singled you out for the mainstream. Freddie Starr and Mike Yarwood had their own vehicles; Lenny Henry's populist take-offs helped him to make a splash on *New Faces*. There was even a quick-fire show entirely devoted to the craft: ITV's *Who Do You Do*?

But whereas most impressionists came out of the old-school club circuit, Bremner came out of public school. He was born in Edinburgh in 1961, and studied French and German at King's College in London. While at university in the early eighties he performed at the Edinburgh Festival and started to get work on radio comedy shows, most notably on that traditional forcing house of new comedy (as well as home to a lot of dodgy material), *Week Ending*. From there his rise was nothing short of stratospheric. He soon had a handful of television jobs. A predictable one doing voices on *Spitting Image*, and a less predictable one on *And There's More*, an ITV show fronted by long-lost showbiz irritant Jimmy Cricket. Then in 1986, at the tender age of 24, he was handed his own BBC2 show, *Now – Something Else*.

Bremner's stock rose steadily, and his shows had higher profile slots each time. He was clearly being groomed for BBC1, and in 1989 used his increasing clout to bring in two performers, John Bird and John Fortune, whose pedigrees stretched back to the early sixties satire boom. This gave

Bremner both credibility and gravitas, and was the point where he started to reassess his position and ambitions. He had always done topical political material, alongside the Barry Norman impressions, but now he became more rigorous, wading through government press releases to unpick the ridiculousness in policy, rather than just going for the funny voices.

His natural home was clearly the more alternative Channel 4, and in 1992 he made the switch, impersonating John Major in a 1993 New Year's Day special, *Rory Bremner ... And the Morning After the Night Before*. The change of channel came about not long after the Conservative Party had a change of leader. The demise of Margaret Thatcher did Bremner's career the power of good. He didn't have the legs to do the Iron Lady and usually called upon the services of Steve Nallon, but Bremner could do John Major in his sleep.

His Channel 4 output established him as this country's preeminent satirist, at a time when satire had fallen out of fashion. Bremner put in a lot of effort to his BAFTA-winning series, *Rory Bremner ... Who Else*? I remember visiting him at his Soho production HQ and seeing his team at work, studying Hansard (the book that contains every word said in Parliament), writing and re-writing material right up to transmission. It looked more like an office in Whitehall, except that I'm not sure if MPs work this hard.

Bremner's regular co-writers were John Langdon and Geoff Atkinson (curious fact: Atkinson was the man behind short-lived satellite channel BSB's sitcom *Heil Honey I'm Home*, which sent up the domestic life of Adolf Hitler). Between them they probably knew the business of the House of Commons better than quite a lot of ministers. The team also had connections: they picked up rumours and whispers that were far too salacious to make it into the papers.

The only thing Bremner seemed to love more than Westminster gossip was cricket, which had even inspired him to have a bash at getting into the charts in 1985, with a parody of Paul Hardcastle's hit '19'. Bremner's version was '19 Not Out' – this feeble number was the allegedly average score by an England batsman during the then recent test against the West Indies. The slap of leather on willow provided him with plenty of material. In the routine featured here, recorded in High Wycombe in the early nineties, when Bremner was cleverly performing the balancing act of being a crowd-pleaser and pamphleteer, he skewers the bluff Yorkshire arrogance of Geoff Boycott with astonishing accuracy.

The shows that Bremner did for Channel 4 were put together with painstaking detail. The star's quick-fire closing monologues alone seemed to feature more characters than an entire series of *Who Do You Do*?, ranging from dishy Des Lynam to newsreader Trevor McDonald, while the Bird/Fortune 'Two Johns' dialogues were inspired portrayals of the bureaucratic doublespeak and corporate gobbledygook, which under New Labour would become better known as 'spin'.

An indication of the esteem Bremner was held in at Channel 4 was the fact that in 1996 he was invited to present the channel's traditional 'Alternative Christmas Message'. Bremner chose to do it as Princess Diana, which caused considerable controversy but lots of nice column inches, although it has to be conceded that Bremner's women have never been quite as convincing as his men. When he did Liberal Democrat leader Paddy Ashdown you could not get a cigarette paper between Bremner and the real thing. His hair-brained weatherman Ian McCaskill was a moment of lunatic beauty. He has a way of capturing the essence of a man and then putting it into cartoon form. Ever since Bremner compared John Prescott to Les Dawson, I've never been able to separate one from the other. Even watching footage on the news in Spring 1996, I thought, 'Is it Dawson or Prescott?'

When New Labour came to power there was a fleeting moment when it looked as if Bremner's satire days might be numbered. After the sleaze and scandal of the Tory Party's final years, surely Tony Blair and co. were too squeaky clean to provide him with much material? Of course, New Labour soon gave Bremner a whole new line in sideswipes, such as portraying robotic control freak Peter Mandelson as a Max Headroom-type animation.

At times it seemed as if politics was making life too easy for Bremner. He could do Tony Blair better than Tony Blair himself – not surprising really, since, like Bremner, Blair was a product of the Scottish public-school system who sounded distinctly English. Bremner also had no problem getting to grips with Gordon Brown's brogue. On the other hand, he had to be on his mettle to keep up with the changes in the Conservative Party. No sooner had he mastered one leader than they were out the back door and another one was in. There must have been a part of the left-leaning Bremner that wished Michael Howard had won the 2005 General Election just so that he could keep doing his faultless, 'I'm not going to hurt you,' patter.

Meanwhile the scripts almost wrote themselves as New Labour revealed that they could be every bit as ludicrous as their predecessors. Financial shenanigans and sexual misde-meanours were just the tip of the iceberg. Bremner also had a field day ripping apart the government's policy on Iraq and Tony Blair's relationship with George Bush.

In fact, just as one might have expected Bremner to rest on his laurels, he has become more hard-hitting than ever. In a recent live show he expressed disappointment with New Labour, saying that Blair had let him down after showing so much promise in 1997, when the PM was 'popular and engaging – like Will Young before the album came out'. Maybe he is turning into the Tony Benn of stand-up, getting more hard-line as his contemporaries soften: 'It is a weird thing, because most people tend to get more conservative as they get older, but I find myself going the opposite way. I am sure that by the end I will be selling Marxist pamphlets on the Holloway Road.'

In 2004, he put his thoughts on the state of the nation and the post 9/11 world into a book, *You are Here*. He was thinking of calling it 'Beyond Parody'. Take the Somerset and Avon police force's campaign against drink driving, sponsored by Threshers: 'Fancy driving around in a squad car with a sticker saying: "Threshers says, Don't drink and drive."' He is clearly a paid-up member of the 'you-couldn't-make-it-up' club. Such stories as the one that Britain did not just sell arms to Iraq, it lent Saddam Hussein the money to buy them, are in danger of putting him out of business.

There is an undeniable echo of Michael Moore in his diligent research, though he insists he is no polemicist – merely stating facts about, for instance, the United States's aggressive foreign policy, rather than trying to be gratuitously provocative. At a reading at the Criterion Theatre he was quick to point out that, for those worried that he was getting serious, 'There is a joke on page 73.' There are, in reality, jokes all through the book, because at heart Bremner still considers himself a comedian, not a campaigner. 'I should always be known as an impressionist and comedian. It is just that what I do now is more topical and political in nature,' he explained in 2005.

As a comedian, however, Bremner occupies a unique position in the landscape. He is the same age as the alternative comedy generation, but apart from his regular support of Comic Relief has never really worked with them. From his early days at King's College, where he did stand-up rather than appear in traditional student revues, Bremner has marched to the beat of his own drum. Yet at the same time he has had a remarkable influence on British comedy.

The television schedules of recent years reflect Bremner's influence. The BBC has had not one, but two impression shows: Alistair McGowan's *Big Impression*, doing the kind of star-puncturing Bremner might well have ended up doing if he had stayed with Auntie, and *Dead Ringers*, mixing celeb put-downs with gentle prods at the likes of Bush and Blair. It is doubtful whether either of these shows would have made it onto our screens without Bremner showing that impressions could work in a post-alternative universe.

At the same time, he is also the respectable face of anti-establishment comedy. The scourge you can invite round for dinner and not expect to complain about human rights in Turkey if you serve kebabs. Mark Thomas, Mark Steel and Jeremy Hardy all have a following but have never become mainstream figures. Robert Newman was in the mainstream as a pin-up stand-up, but having reinvented himself as a satirist he has been marginalized again.

It is to Bremner's enduring credit that he manages to get his ideas across and maintain his high profile. He is clearly doing something right – in 2005 there were reports that Gordon Brown had asked him to write gags for him. The reason may have been that the outwardly dour Chancellor wanted to pep up his image, but there may also have been a feeling in the New Labour camp that it is better to have someone like Bremner in the New Labour tent pissing out than outside pissing in.

And so, after 25 years, Bremner continues to be a thorn in the establishment's side. Maybe even a sharper one than when he started out. Don't be fooled by the fact that he has recently been sighted on the BBC captaining a team on the gently topical game show *Mock the Week*. He could stick a ferret up your trouser leg at any moment.

Bruce Dessau

'John Major'

Wycombe Swan, Buckinghamshire (1994),
Laughing Stock LAFFC 30

'Golly! Well, it hasn't exactly been a dull
year, has it?

But I think amidst all the froth and
babble, amidst all the furore and the
brouhaha, I think we're forgetting
something rather important: I'm still here.

[*Laughter*]

To govern the country as I have done for
the last two years takes a lot of nerve.
Getting out of a recession that was none of
our doing, by abandoning policies that were
none of our responsibility, in favour of
ideas in which none of us is confident,
that takes a lot of nerve, Madam President.

I have that nerve. And I'm still here …

They said it couldn't be done. It wasn't.

[*Laughter*]

They said I wasn't up to the job. I'm not.

[*Laughter*]

They said things couldn't get any worse.
They have.

[*Laughter*]

But I'm still here.

49

So let us get back to basics, back to basics, the big idea that will finally answer all those who say to me, 'John, what's the big idea?'

[*Laughter*]

What I wunt, what I wunt is to see standards of decency and honesty that apply all the way from the bottom of society, right the way up to not quite the top.

Why should we give money to teenage single mothers when that money would be better spent building prisons to house their delinquent children?

[*Laughter*]

Two years ago, British industry was nowhere. Today, it's all over the place.

I did that.

[*Laughter and applause*]

Everywhere you go, let there be no doubt, let there be no doubt, everywhere you go, factories are humming with activity as the official receiver goes about his business.

[*Laughter*]

And so let us put the blame where it belongs.

With the Germans,

With the Danes,

With the Rebels,

With the Bastards,

And above all, not with me.

Because I'm still here, you're still there, and everything's going to be all right. Thank you.

[*Laughter and applause*]

'Michael Heseltine'

Wycombe Swan, Buckinghamshire (1994),
Laughing Stock LAFFC 30

VOICEOVER

Story time, read today by the President of
the Board of Trade, the Right Honourable
Michael Heseltine, MP.

BREMNER

[*As Heseltine*] Once upon a time, not so
very long ago, there lived a very brave and
handsome prince. He was loved throughout
the land for his bravery, his golden locks,
and for his interventionist policy in the
industrial sector. And there was also
living in the land at that time a wicked
witch who held the whole country in her
thrall.

[*Laughter*]

No one dare challenge her, for those who
incurred her displeasure would be banished
forever and forced to spend more time with
their family.

[*Laughter*]

As time went by, the wicked witch grew into
an evil and capricious dragon. The people
suffered greatly. They longed to be rid of
her, and their suffering reached the ears
of the handsome prince who was living in
exile in the forest. He could contain
himself no longer. Rising up and gathering

together all his strength, which was considerable, he took up arms and slew the wicked dragon.

Hurrah, cried the people.

Hurrah!

Here is surely a prince to lead us into the nineties and beyond.

[*Laughter*]

 But I have to tell you, there was also living at the palace at that time one of the poor boys from the village …

[*Laughter*]

He was a runty little chap and many did not even know his name. As the wicked dragon lay dying, she called out to him. Small boy! Who is the fairest of them all? You are, he said, his fingers tightly crossed behind his grubby little back.

[*Laughter*]

And do you know what the people did? I'll tell you what they bloody did. They only went and made the little boy king.

[*Laughter*]

Of all the ungrateful things to do, after all the prince had done for them. And what did the small boy do? He palmed the prince off with a servant's job. Well, thank you very much indeed, small boy.

[*Laughter*]

Thank you very much indeed, you long streak of not very much at all.

With your citizen's charter and your classless society, with your 'cone charter' and your trips to Ikea and your stone cladding and your Banoffee pie.

[*Laughter*]

And so it was that they all lived happy ever after.

For the first few weeks.

For then, things began to go terribly …

Disastrously …

WONDERFULLY …

Wrong.

[*Laughter and applause*]

'Prince Charles'

Wycombe Swan, Buckinghamshire (1994),
Laughing Stock LAFFCD 107

[*As Prince Charles*] I had a very
disappointing tour of Australia. They
always ask me, 'What do the royal family
miss most about Australia?'

And I say, 'The rent.'

[*Laughter*]

'I went to this place called Parramatta in
the outback. I … I felt a bit embarrassed,
because I was wearing a fur cap. It was my
mother's fault. I said to her, 'I'm going
to Parramatta …' She said, 'Wear the fox
hat.'

[*Laughter*]

[*As himself*] Anyone got a satellite dish in
High Wycombe? Are you allowed them? Are you
allowed satellite dishes? Do you have to
have the stone cladding as well? [*Laughter*]
Because it's usually compulsory, isn't it?

I mean, because I … I bought a Sky dish so
I could actually watch the adverts, and
they keep interrupting the adverts and
showing test match cricket.

[*Laughter*]

No, it's true, and every now and again you
get a thing called static interference.

Except with Sky it's not static interference, it's Geoffrey Boycott.

[*As Geoffrey Boycott*] Now, the thing about Brian Lara ... [Laughter] Two things wrong ... He gets too many runs and he scores them too quickly.

[*Laughter*]

Don't have to score runs in a test match. Not about scoring runs. It's about staying in the wicket ...

[*Laughter*]

Draw test matches. Don't have to win them. Only one-day games you have to win. No, you can draw, because people say cricket's a team game. That's bollocks. Is that.

[*Laughter*]

Its about one man and ten people trying to help you improve your average.

[*Laughter*]

'The Queen'

Queens Theatre, Edinburgh (1998),
Laughing Stock LAFFCD 99

[*As the Queen*] My subjects, looking back over last year, the overwhelming sense is one of great loss, the loss that we all suffered. And looking back over the photographs, one is struck by the fact that wherever she went she made people happy.

Thousands, indeed hundreds of thousands of people who would turn up to greet her wherever she went, and would turn up to wave her goodbye as she left … And on that fateful day, last year, when we gathered to say goodbye to her for the last time, I turned to my husband and said:

'We're going to miss that yacht you know …'

[*Laughter and applause*]

[*As himself*] The royal family are desperately trying to keep up with the times now. There's a new switchboard at Buckingham Palace you can ring up. It says, *'Hello, you're through to Buckingham Palace. If you want to marry Charles, please press 1 now. If you want to marry Edward, please press 2. If you're a Catholic, please replace the handset and try again.'*

[*Laughter*]

They're even on the Internet. And Alan Bennett's on the Internet now. Alan Bennett on the Internet, *[As Alan Bennett]* oh that'll be the day. Signed Alan here at Betty's dot, the tearooms, dot, uk.

[*Laughter*]

[*As himself*] What's the royal family's website? Does anybody know? The royalfamily@loggerheads.co.uk?

[*Laughter*]

You've still got Prince Philip, the world's greatest diplomat wandering around in the background. It's fabulous. They went to India to Amritsar, the scene of that terrible Indian massacre, and Philip's going around. He looks at the bullet holes in the walls. 'Oh look here, missed a few then!' I don't know how many were killed but it got to lunch time and he was going, 'Come on, come on, come on; I could murder an Indian.'

[*Laughter*]

And the next generation, Camilla. Camilla could be Queen next year and we haven't a clue what she sounds like. Do you know what she sounds like? I haven't a clue. I want to see her on the chat show circuit.

[*As Clive James*] And now … ha, ha, ha, ha … thank you Mr Mitsubishi, wishy washy, plenty doshy.

[*Laughter*]

And now it's time to meet the woman for whom lese majesty means wham, bam, thank you Your Royal Highness. As we say, hail, God save the Queen and how was it for you Camilla … Parker … Bowles.

[*Laughter*]

Camilla, why is it that Charles has kept you out of the public eye for so long?

[*Long pause, then in a very deep cockney male voice*] Well I don't really know really.

[*Laughter and applause*]

I suppose he's got 'is reasons hasn't 'e ?.

[*Continued laughter*]

[*As himself*] Because they've got to be familiar, I mean a lot of the familiar voices I used to do, they're all retiring, or gone into retirement …

[*As Peter Alliss*] Ooh, well, well, well. Well this funny old game of stick and ball. It drives you mad on occasions. As my old caddy used to say, 'You drive for show and you putt for dough …' I wonder if he's watching now, the old chap? Old Jimmy McTouchy. He's probably there in the old leather armchair at the 16th, a glass of Glenfiddich in his hand. 'I hope the leg's better, and er, and er, regards to Elspeth. I hope she's recovering from that bit of trouble with the old angina, and er..'

[*Laughter*]

But the great warm voices, the Cliff Morgans of this world …

[*As Cliff Morgan*] You know you can say this about sportsmen, it's not about characters any more; it's not about winning. It's about getting together in the showers, and a little rub down with the nail brush … But people used to play with great heart and with soul. And I think of the great players like Martina Navratilova-lova-lova-love-lova-lova. You know, she had heart, she had soul; she had balls, didn't she …?

[*Laughter*]

[*As himself*] A lot of the people I know are from the world of cricket, and a number of my friends are down in England; there's Allan Lamb who played cricket for England and was born in South Africa. But he gets things slightly wrong. He tried to get me to do a charity show the other day. It was a cystic fibrosis thing and he rang up and said:

[*As Lamb, in a heavy South African accent*] Hey Roy, I want to do this little show for septic halitosis

[*Laughter*]

[*As himself*] He's trying to get hold of John McCarthy …

[*As Lamb*] Who is that bloke who was held hostage in Debenhams?

[*Laughter*]

That Paul McCartney bloke? Yeah, that's him. I tell you, they don't bloody take any pensioners over there do they? Who was that bloke they held with him? You know, the one with the beard, Terry Wogan?

[*Laughter*]

[*As himself*] And he was out in Cape Town and wondering if he could get Nelson Mandela to do a golf day. Imagine the phone call …

[*As Lamb*] Hey … Nelson?, it's Lambie here. Do you think you could do my golf day for me?

[*As Nelson Mandela*] Er … listen Lambie, I was held in prison for 30 years in a cell that was 10 foot by 2 foot. You think I can't bloody putt? You bet your arse!

[*Laughter and applause*]

4. ARNOLD BROWN

Of course, nowadays it's more PLC ...

You want the Zelig of modern comedy? The man who has always been there with a quip for every occasion? Look no further than Arnold Brown. The droll Glaswegian stand-up was there at the very first night of the Comedy Store on 19 May 1979. He arrived on stage on the brink of a new era. And, about forty seconds later he left, gonged off by an audience baying for blood.

Since then this impeccably laconic grandfather of modern comedy has seen other comedians come and go. Some have skulked back to their jobs in middle management, others have ended up filling Wembley Arena. Arnold has seen it all. He has supported Frank Sinatra and lived to tell the tale. And being both Scottish and Jewish he is a member of two important comedy clans. Or as Brown puts it: 'Two ethnic minorities for the price of one. Perhaps the best value in the West End tonight ... Perhaps not ...'

Arnold Brown became a performer unusually late. He was already 42 when he made his memorable debut at the Comedy Store. Up to that point he had been an accountant, first in Glasgow, where this son of a greengrocer was born in 1936, before moving to north London in 1963. But as he explained to me over tea in central London in April 2006 he had always been a comedian in his head even when he wasn't doing it for a living.

'I was a fan of *That Was the Week That Was*, the Pythons, Billy Connolly and Dave Allen, but my biggest influence was

Woody Allen, particularly his Jewish angst and insecurity, which I identified with. I remember laughing at his early films such as *Sleeper* when there was practically no-one but me there in the cinema. Then that Jewish thing overlapped with a Glaswegian thing. I admired the great surreal Scottish comedian Chic Murray. I wasn't influenced by him but he struck a chord with me. My two obsessions all my life have been Jewishness and Scottishness.'

Murray, who died in 1985, was a master of the droll, absurd gag. 'He's going along the road and a passer-by says to him, "Is that the moon up there?" And Murray replies, "I'm sorry I don't know. I'm a stranger round here myself."' Brown sees Murray as an upholder of a Caledonian tradition of intelligent comedy. 'In Glasgow there is a flirtation with ideas and the surreal. Maybe it's a Celtic thing. You also get it in Liverpool. You can actually do concepts and leaps of the imagination. Some of my lines are a homage to him – homage meaning plagiarism: I was walking along the street and I walked into a lamppost. It was so dark inside that lamppost I decided to walk out again.' Murray is hugely important in Glasgow comedy history, and even had an influence on fellow shipyard escapee Billy Connolly. Both had respect for the potency of language.

Brown claims he, 'drifted into comedy like other people drift into crime,' mucking about and taping material at home and being the funny one with his mates. But in the late sixties he made a concerted effort to find a way in, going on a comedy writing course taught by Brad Ashton, who used to write for acts for comedians ranging from perma-tanned light entertainment duo Mike and Bernie Winters to Groucho Marx. 'I learned about the construction of lines and that was why I zoned in on Woody Allen – it was the rhythm and the craft. His moose routine is still the funniest routine ever. Not a word is wasted.'

Brown started to send gags into radio and television shows, and by the turn of the decade was picking up work on

BBC Radio 4's topical show *Week Ending*. In 1971 he even managed to get a sketch into a show fronted by comedy legend Ronnie Barker, entitled 'Lines From my Grandfather's Forehead'. But it was the politically turbulent mid-seventies that kick-started Brown's comedy career.

'Until then I'd been writing jokes as a hobby, but when we started working a three-day week in the office because of the energy crisis I had time to concentrate.' The sense of humour is like a muscle and the more you have time to exercise it the stronger it becomes. *Week Ending* started to accept more of his material and he found he could come up with topical jokes quicker than ever.

Performing, however, was another matter. He had never done it, never really even thought about it. Then one day in the spring of 1979 he heard about a new comedy club opening at 69 Dean Street in Soho, started by two Englishmen, old-school stand-up comedian Don Ward and life-insurance salesman Peter Rosengard, who had seen a similar club on a trip to America. Anyone could have a go, but if the audience didn't like them they'd be gonged off by resident host Alexei Sayle. Brown immediately applied.

He landed a booking along with countless other wannabes but soon realized that he didn't know anything about stage-craft. 'I thought you improvised, so I did my opening joke – "I'm an accountant, I check things …Can you hear me at the back?" But somebody shouted out, "We can't hear you at the back," before I got to my punch line and I was gonged off.' Brown failed miserably but suddenly felt at home on stage. 'I came back the next night despite public demand.'

His gags were like depth charges or time-release pills – you had to think before you laughed. Brown really eked out his jokes, and in the process turned the pause into an art form. Interestingly his writing mentor Brad Ashton had been at school with master of the meaningful silence Harold Pinter in the 1930s; if Pinter had gone into stand-up he might have resembled Brown (curious fact: Pinter actually did write some sketches for an early show with Peter Cook – and reputedly put in lots of pauses because he was paid by the minute rather than the word).

One cannot underestimate how brave this kind of style was in front of a lager-crazed late-night audience. Contrast it with Ben Elton who came along a couple of years later and specifically developed a breathless Gatling Gun delivery, because he knew if he ever stopped for breath the hecklers would have a chance to wipe the floor with him. Brown kept coming back, and one night in 1979 his style just clicked. Instead of being heckled or gonged off, he hit his stride and the next thing he knew he'd been riffing for forty minutes. He definitely now had a proper act. And just to confirm it, fellow comic Keith Allen argued with the management to make them pay Brown his £10 fee for the first time.

The Comedy Store quickly became a phenomenon, unleashing alternative comedy on the world. Television crews would come down and film the queues outside. Celebrities such as Dustin Hoffman and Jack Nicholson would drop in to check it out. Like everybody else they had to squeeze into the tiny lift which only held six people and work their way up to the club. Brown could see a scene and a stance forming. Non-sexist, non-racist humour was the order of the day. The age of political correctness, or PC comedy, had arrived. 'Other comedy groups such as the *Not the Nine O'Clock News* teams were irreverent and anti-everything and apolitical, but this group was very political, very left wing and anti-Margaret Thatcher, who has just become prime minister.'

Eventually the acts that were gaining the most publicity decided to go it alone. Comedian Peter Richardson found a new venue above the nearby Raymond's Revue Bar and dubbed it the Comic Strip in a wry reference to the women who took their clothes off for a living below. In October 1980, he set up a regular ensemble featuring himself and Nigel Planer, Rik Mayall and Ade Edmondson, with Alexei Sayle as compere. Dawn French and Jennifer Saunders came along a few months later but Brown was in the Comic Strip from the start, despite being very different to these excitable young turks.

'I performed a important purpose because of the pace of the show. Everyone else was over the top, I just did 50 one-liners in 17 minutes. You had to work them out. I always remember the gaps then the laughter.' The source of Brown's material was autobiographical, referring to his Scottishness or his Jewishness, and harking back to his tenement youth or alluding to his current residence in lush Hampstead 'NW Twee', where even the council house tenants had second council houses in the country.

His material might seem almost mainstream now, but at the time it had a surprisingly radical edge in a world of fictional, 'My mother-in-law is so fat she kick starts Concorde,' cracks. 'When I see a comedian I like to know who they are and where they are from or I feel cheated. I believe in comedy as truth.' Not that he wasn't averse to bending the facts a little. 'I used to say in my act at the Comic Strip, "Next door, as you listen to my jokes, 192 Japanese businessmen are lusting over our women and you are sitting here doing nothing about it."'

Another thing that singled Brown out, apart from being twenty years older than his colleagues, was his catchphrase. No-one but he had one. From a very early stage he used to end sentences with the simple three-word mantra, 'And why not.' To this day, Brown is not sure how it happened, but he thinks that maybe there is a deep-seated reason for it. 'My real name is Abraham Arnold Lizerbram. I'd changed it when I became an accountant.' Maybe when he stood on stage and said, 'My name is Arnold Brown … and why not?' there was a sense of quiet defiance. Why shouldn't he change his name if he wanted to?

As the Comic Strip took off, the younger acts were snapped up by television, going on to become household names after BBC2's *The Young Ones* and Channel 4's *Comic Strip* films.

Brown made a couple of appearances on their shows but slightly missed the boat. 'I was still getting my act together. I had a great time though when the Comic Strip went on tour: there were no agents, no managers, no rules. They were innocent times. It was very PC, of course nowadays it's more PLC. I set up a club in the Pentameters pub in Hampstead and wanted to book Ben Elton, Rik Mayall, French and Saunders, Nigel Planer and Peter Richardson. It sounds ridiculous now but the landlady was reluctant. She said, "I'll give it a try ..."'

He continued to work and had a couple more stabs at television in the early eighties, most notably in the Channel 4 series *Interference*. But most of the time he focused on live shows. Jongleurs had set up its first club in Battersea in South London. 'It was a fantastic place to work in before the yuppies came along. I can remember Paul Merton and Jeremy Hardy and I having a wonderful time there.' He soon became a master of slow burn stand-up, who could even turn a lukewarm response to his advantage. 'I don't like too much applause at the start. That's how fascism began.'

Brown gained more experience taking shows to the Edinburgh Fringe Festival. In 1983 and 1984 – the year he finally gave up accountancy – he did shows with fellow deadpan maestro Norman Lovett. In 1985 Paul Merton and Nick Revell joined them. In 1986 his show was called Arnold Brown and Co and featured special guests such as a very young Harry Hill. Then in 1987 he did a show called Brown Blues, with music provided by cabaret duo Barb Jungr and Michael Parker.

The show had been getting good feedback and good reviews, but it still came as a surprise when towards the end of the run the show was interrupted by someone walking on stage and presenting Brown with a bunch of flowers. It was not a secret admirer but a member of the Perrier Award committee telling Brown that he was the winner.

Compared to today, with the Perrier (recently replaced by the Eddies) regarded as the biggest, most prestigious award in comedy, the prize was decidedly low-key. 'There was a small party at a discreet hotel in Charlotte Square, broadcaster Miles Kington made a speech, we had some wine then photographs were taken and all went home.' But Brown's victory marked a watershed in Perrier Award history, and the tipping point in comedy when the underground went over ground.

Until then, Perrier winners had come via the fringe theatre circuit rather than the alternative comedy world. There weren't even that many eligible shows for the judges to see. Brown was the first stand-up to win the Award who could truly be defined as part of comedy's new wave. From this point on alternative comedians would dominate the Edinburgh Fringe, and the Perrier Awards would become an essential stepping stone on the path to success.

After Arnold's victory, television would be quick to snap up talent. By the early nineties, Frank Skinner, Lee Evans and Steve Coogan would all proudly count themselves as Perrier winners, but it was Arnold that sparked the important modern trend of one man and a mike (aided by some songs, admittedly) making off with the prize rather than earnest drama students temporarily muscling in on the comedy business until a better offer from the National Theatre came along.

Even back then, before comedy was red-hot, Brown's career got an important boost. 'I got my own series on BBC Radio 4 and more voiceovers. I did a pilot for a BBC2 sitcom called *The Brown Man*. And it helped me get my biggest gig to date, supporting Frank Sinatra at Glasgow Rangers Ibrox Football Ground on 10 July 1990. Sixteen years on he is typically modest about it. 'Who else could they have got? Billy Connolly was probably too big, Jerry Sadowitz? Well it, was a middle-aged audience, I think they needed someone safer than Sadowitz and I was the best bet.' Brown never met old blue eyes but still got a famous if fictional gag out of it. 'I suggested Frank should open the show with "Fly Me to Dunoon".'

Brown is a quietly passionate comedy obsessive who can talk for hours about humour. When he talks about Scottish comedy, however, he is really talking about Glasgow comedy. For him, there have been few great comics to emerge out of Edinburgh – Ronnie Corbett is a small exception rather than the rule, and the heart of Scottish comedy is the west coast. 'Glaswegians can take an idea and run with it. They don't need their jokes on a plate.'

There is something about the city that makes it the perfect cradle for comedy. 'I think the rich social mix has lent itself to humour,' suggests Brown. 'You had the mix of Protestants and Catholics in the streets, then also the Highlanders coming in and the Jewish immigrants, replaced later by the Asian community. Jews always gravitate to urban conurbations. It's a combination you don't get anywhere else.' He sees himself as part of a triumvirate of contemporary Scots humorists, along with the late, great Ivor Cutler and Jerry Sadowitz. All are Jewish, and both Brown and Cutler were born within a hundred yards of Rangers football ground.

Brown has his own theory about why Jews dominate comedy. 'They have always asked deep philosophical questions from the very start, and when they were expelled from other countries the displacement made them look at things as outsiders. Because of their circumstances they saw things differently and criticized them. Look at American comedy – Jewish comedians defined it, from Jack Benny, Mel Brooks and Sid Caesar to Woody Allen and Jerry Seinfeld. Back in Scotland, Ivor, Jerry and I were the weird ones seeing things that others take for granted.'

He thinks that his humour derives from the perspective of Jewish Talmudic justice that identifies itself emphatically with the underdog, attacking only the powerful and those in charge of our lives. 'Lenny Bruce was for me the quintessential example of this Hebrew tradition.'

If Cutler was more surreal and Sadowitz better at saying the unsayable, Brown's dry, self-deprecating style enabled him to update the traditional Jewish stereotype. 'When I was ten my friend told me that all Jewish people are wealthy. I remember that day even now, running home excitedly to break the news to my mother and father and we spent that weekend taking up the floorboards.'

Nearly thirty years after his stand-up debut, Arnold Brown is still working hard and still has ambitions: 'I'm the comedian's comedian but my real ambition is to become the bank manager's comedian.' He still gigs regularly at home and abroad and has a Radio 4 sitcom in development, entitled *The Insecurity Man*, in which he plays a security guard. His next project is a comic novella inspired by his mythical Uncle Harry's obsession with the history of Jewish humour.

Comedy is not the sort of career that you retire from. Perhaps it retires you by not giving you any work any more, but there is no sign of that happening with Arnold Brown. His career is more varied than he might ever have expected. In 2003 he even did his bit for the Scottish film industry, with a cameo in the Ewan McGregor movie *Young Adam*. The grandfather of modern comedy has no plans to quit. He takes a final sip of tea, raises one eyebrow and concludes by coming as close as it is possible to come to revealing why he does what he does: 'I'm still trying to get the attention I didn't get as an adult.'

Bruce Dessau

'The Secret of Comedy'

Assembly Rooms, Edinburgh (1991),
Laughing Stock LAFFC 04

People ask me about the secret of comedy.
Well, the secret of great comedy is timing.
For example, you the audience come here
tonight, and I arrive one week later;
that's bad timing.

[*Laughter*]

I'm a hardened professional; I've noticed
it makes a difference even one day out. My
father was a late developer and I had the
unique pleasure of watching him grow up …
It was embarrassing, I learnt to walk
before he did.

He was also addicted to cigarettes, and I
always saw him behind a puff of smoke. You
know, until the age of ten, I thought that
he was a professional magician. And he
thought I was his son.

[*Laughter*]

We had the shame in Glasgow of my father
being a teetotaller, and the disgrace on
Saturday nights of him being thrown into
pubs.

Of course, I now live in Hampstead, London,
NW Twee.

It's so radical chic there; so radical
chic. We have low-alcohol lager louts. And
the people in council houses have got a

second council house in Wales they go to at
the weekend.

[*Laughter*]

And why not? We have organizations like the
Campaign for Real Champagne. And our
version of Exit, the society for voluntary
euthanasia, is called, 'Ciao' …

[*Laughter*]

The other week I wanted to listen to a wide
variety of music, so I wandered into a
supermarket … And I wanted to get a loaf
of, of wholemeal bread, and they only did
white bread. I was disappointed. Well, to
be honest I was crying. Men cry too, look
at Edward Heath.

[*Laughter*]

And I was about to leave the supermarket
with my white bread and I noticed,
strangely enough, a cardboard cut out and
it was a farmer type. You know that type
with the, the white smock, the red cheeks,
the big grin, the bushy eyebrows; the kind
of person you would run away from at a
party.

[*Laughter*]

And I noticed a very strange thing: from
one of his eyes a tear was coming down, a
tear …

And I looked down at my white bread and
suddenly my white bread was being converted
into wholemeal bread. Today that

supermarket is a shrine. Pilgrims come from all over the world with wheelchairs packed with ham waiting to be cured.

[*Laughter and groans*]

I do remember, sometime in the distant past, I was in a supermarket, I don't know where, and I was in time to catch that ritual when they don't know the price of an item at the checkout counter. And the woman behind the checkout counter was holding a large box of Ariel washing powder in the air and she was shouting out, she was definitely shouting out, 'Marie, Marie, Marie!'

But no Marie …

The queue was getting bigger and bigger at the checkout counter. What happened was this. The responsibility of being the only person in the supermarket to know the price of every item had got to Marie. She had locked herself in the washroom and she was throwing up. She'd obviously waffled at the interview …

[*Laughter*]

'Marie, at peak time we have to identify the price of every item very quickly and efficiently, can you do that?' 'Oh, no bother at all Mr Robertson …'

[*Laughter*]

Anyway, I wandered away from the fracas. Whenever I have a fracas in front of me I always wander away. I don't like trouble, and trouble doesn't like me.

And you know, it is strange, when you wander down some parts of the supermarket, you find a quiet corner. It's very, very spiritual isn't it? You don't see anyone coming this way or that way, and the fantasy is that, you know, you might be locked in with all these serving suggestions.

I saw a very strange sight. In one of the rows of the shelves, all the sell-by dates on the items had been left blank. I thought to myself, how very existential: possibly infinity … I had a quick chat with the manager; and it turned out to be part time work in the holidays by philosophy students.

[*Laughter*]

That's all they're fit for, isn't it?

Then there was another fracas at the checkout counter. This time it was three of them at the checkout counter, holding up some garden furniture. Three of them. And it was like an Olympic event.

[*Laughter*]

They're trying to hold up the garden furniture, it was like synchronized holding up of garden furniture. And they were all shouting out together, 'Marie, Marie for God's sake, Marie,' and because there were three of them jumping up and down, they looked like the Nolan sisters.

[*Laughter*]

The whole atmosphere of the supermarket turned into Mardi Gras. People started dancing with each other. It was the first time I had personally done a tango with a store detective. At the end of it, I found my wallet was missing …

[*Laughter*]

Marie eventually heard the noise and she rushed out, and she was killed … Crushed under the garden furniture …

[*Laughter*]

But there is a little plaque to Marie on the side of the checkout counter: 'To Marie, who died so that we could sit in the sun.'

Who says there's no sentiment in big business ?

There's so much pressure nowadays. The other week I went to see my doctor. And I was in the waiting room and I decided to pass the time finishing a novel, but the other patients complained about the noise of the typewriter.

[*Laughter*]

You know, the role of the artist in this country is desperate. When I got in to see the doctor he wasn't doing anything, anything medical; he was actually listening

to a Chris de Burgh record. Well someone's
got to do it.

[*Laughter*]

And when he saw me come in he stopped
listening to the record and he started
listening to my heart, and he recommended
that I should make an album. He said that I
had a very commercial beat.

[*Laughter*]

Then he said, 'Arnold' — we're on first
name terms, I call him 'Doctor' — he said,
'Arnold, I've got some terrible news for
you: there's just been a terrible plane
crash in the United States of America.' I
said, 'What's that got to do with me …?' He
said to me, 'How can you be so callous?' He
said, 'Arnold, I've got some terrible news
for you personally, you've only got 40
years to live.' I said, 'Can I have a
second opinion, Doctor?' He said, 'Well it
could be 60 years if you become a private
patient …'

[*Laughter*]

1955, and Albert Einstein and Marilyn
Monroe were starting an affair, and I was
hiding in the cupboard (it was a Greyhound
bus trip that had gone wrong) and I was
looking at them and noticing every detail.
And Marilyn said to Albert: 'I think I'll
put on a record.' And she put on the record
of T.S. Eliot reading *The Waste Land*.

And they started dancing to it. I couldn't believe my eyes. I could not believe my eyes … And I heard her say: 'Albert, my little itsy-bitsy Nobel prize winner, my 200-page entry in *Who's Who*. You're a man of the world, tell me about Glasgow.' She said, 'Tell me about Glasgow.'

And he said, 'What are you talking about?' She said, 'Tell me about the bigotry, tell me everything about the football teams …'

[*Laughter*]

And Albert said, 'I know nothing about it.' Then Marilyn said, 'I'm only kidding, I'm only pulling your leg … What I really want to know, tell me about the theory of relativity; explain to me the theory of relativity.' And he leaned forward (and I had to lean forward myself to catch it), and he said, 'I'm sorry Marilyn, I never go that far on a first date …'

'Men's Magazines'

Komedia Club, Brighton, (2001),
Laughing Stock LAFFCD 0127

Sex is everywhere, except when you need it. And Freud never told us that, did he? And, you know, men are in crisis.

Look at him. [*Points at man in the audience*]

[*Laughter*].

You see, men are in crisis because, basically, their roles are changing. Sometimes they're not even, you know, the breadwinner.

Sexually, they're still unsure of themselves, their performance. They really are in crisis. Every week of the year is designated to headline an issue, but, for lots of men, every week is Breast Awareness Week.

[*Laughter*]

And you can see part of the problem if you just go into any newsagents, and there on the top shelf you see these men's magazines.

Now, they're on the top shelf, I suppose, on the premise that small people wouldn't be interested.

You go in there, you might even see on the top shelf, Asian Babes. Asian Babes.

I wouldn't like to go into W.H. Smith and see on the top shelf — Hebrew Lovelies.

'Oh, can I have a copy of Hebrew Lovelies please?'

'It's not for me, it's for my Rabbi'

[*Laughter*].

And the men's magazines are very, very life-diminishing — fast cars, guns, all that kind of thing.

Now, women are a much more evolved species. I read women's magazines now and then.

But the strange thing about women's magazines, there're so many of them — hundreds of these women's magazines. I mean, like *Belle*, *Marie Claire*, *Essentials*, *Glamour*, *Us*, *Them*, *You*. I hear there's a new magazine coming out that's called *You — No, not you, the woman standing behind you*.

[*Laughter*].

So they are catering for everyone.

On television they have much sex and, you know that series Ally McBeal, you know, that genetically modified American, and the theme of the programme was three in a bed.

We had that in Glasgow years ago. We called it overcrowding.

In some parts of the country, people do certain sexual things with sheep. Pretty, pretty disgusting. But I want to remind you tonight, we also, we also *eat* sheep. We eat sheep.

But the point is, we never give the sheep the choice.

'Do you want to be eaten, or made love to?'

I know what I'd say. And when you think about it, after a few minutes of pain, it will have its whole life to look forward to.

Now, I was coming from Edinburgh during the festival, back to London, and I looked out the window of the train and saw this field of sheep, and I was looking at them, and they looked very attractive, very attractive.

Very friendly and warm, nice, and, you know, very come hither. And in some cases, you know, the sheep's coat rises up high on the neck, and it's very much like a dress worn by Shirley Bassey at a film premier. And the thought entered my head, maybe they're asking for it …

[*Laughter*]

I was in Soho the other week, I wanted to make a telephone call, and I don't like portable phones.

The people who use them are impervious to the way that they affect other people, selfish people, crass people. I must admit though, the mobile phone is a terrific advance.

I mean, I can still remember that we were the first family in the street to have *cordless pyjamas*. And the neighbours gave a party for us — how do they keep up?

[*Laughter*]

So, I was making this phone call in one of these telephone kiosks in Soho, and, as you know, inside they're all filled with all these sex services cards, and one in particular caught my eye, it was Authentic Dungeon. Authentic Dungeon.

And I thought to myself, here's a history graduate who's gone off the rails. I mean, four years of study and you end up being an advisor to the porn industry.

[*Laughter*]

And so the card listed all the services, humiliation, bondage, and correction. No reference to New Labour. And it referred to cages, racks, nail beds, and at the bottom of it was a little line that said, 'We Guarantee Complete Releif'.

So I picked up the phone and I phoned them up. 'Hello, is that the Authentic Dungeon service?' And a very educated voice said, 'Oh, hello. Yes, it is.'

And I said, 'I'm disgusted.' 'Disgusted,' I said'.

And he said, 'What are you talking about?'

I said, 'The spelling – relief is 'i' before 'e' except after 'c'. And I put the phone down.

I think it's so important to fight illiteracy whenever you find it.

Now this is a tip kind of show – the whole show is a tip. And here's a tip for gardeners.

The best way to lay compost, in my opinion, just in my opinion, is to get someone else to do it.

[*Laughter*]

'Life Tips'

Komedia Club, Brighton (2001),
Laughing Stock LAFFCD 0127

[*Applause*]

I must say …

I must say something.

I must say that I don't like too much applause at the beginning, that's how fascism started …

[*Laughter*]

And some of you are probably too young to know what fascism is.

How can I describe it …?

It's like Portishead with flags.

[*Laughter*]

You're probably surprised to know that I even know who Portishead are.

I don't.

I do all my research from posters.

[*Laughter*]

You know sometimes you have no access to classical music; you just happen to be out and about and you feel like hearing some classical music.

Phone up the Gas Board.

[*Laughter*]

83

A couple of warnings about, about drugs. Drugs can be very, very difficult. I don't take drugs myself; I always put them back.

But, as I told a musician friend of mine who takes drugs, I told him if you take drugs it can lead onto terrible things …

Like jazz.

[*Laughter*]

I was walking down streets of London the other week and a man came up to me and said: *'can you spare a deposit – on a small studio flat in Camden Town?'*

I couldn't. But I was so glad to see the man had his aspirations.

[*Laughter*]

Cut to another scene: in my home town of Glasgow a few months ago another man came up to me and said: *'Have you got a meat pie on you, Jimmy?'*

Compare the aspirations.

[*Laughter*]

Why do we get into comedy? Because we're different. We've been forced to look at life in a different way because we're Scottish, we're Jewish, we're black, we're gay or, in some cases like Jim Davidson, we're not funny.

We get into comedy, and we are shaped by our childhood. I remember growing up in Glasgow – this is sad. My father had a

stutter — this is true. And I say that
without any hesitation whatsoever …

[*Laughter*]

One day he told me, he said, 'Arnold, never
say boo to a goose.' I always remember
that, and it did puzzle me. You see, in our
neighbourhood there was no opportunity to
say boo to such an animal …

[*Laughter*]

5. STEVE COOGAN

I pay taxes to let them pretend to be trees …

Most character comedians would be deliriously happy if they created one iconic figure in their career. Steve Coogan can claim at least two. There is Alan Partridge, of course, whose life is one long spiral into bleak, blazered despair. Partridge seems to dog Coogan – just when you think he's shaken his alter ego off, back he comes again. There has even been talk of a Partridge movie one day.

And then there is Paul Calf, who actually predates Partridge by a fistful of years. Music producers talk about the man who turned down the Beatles; the television industry should talk about the network that turned down a certain trio of comedians. In the late eighties, Granada Television spotted three performers who were making gentle waves on the Mancunian comedy circuit and put them into a modest shoe-string sketch show. There must have been a hope that this would be picked up by national television and propel these people to greater heights. Sadly, it went no further. But the stars certainly did. They were John Thomson, Caroline Aherne and Steve Coogan.

One of the characters Coogan did on this lost show was a drunken, student-hating lager lout, originally called, as if he had just tumbled out of the pages *Viz*, Duncan Disorderly. I first came across this 'politically-incorrect-in-every-way' creation when Coogan won the Perrier Award with John Thomson in 1992. Coogan had previously been making a comfortable living doing voiceovers for adverts – 'horrible acrylic sweaters only £3.99!' He also specialized in mainstream impressions – he did Margaret Thatcher on *Spitting Image* and I remember him doing a very wooden, i.e. very good, Roger Moore on *Pebble Mill at One* in 1988. But having decided that he didn't want to be the next Bobby Davro, he shrewdly repackaged himself as a hipper, cooler alternative model.

Coogan's Edinburgh hit was not so much a show, more a comedic CV, with the star demonstrating that he could inhabit a wide range of characters, from crap comedian Duncan Thickett to cosmically awful sports commentator Alan Partridge. And in the middle there was this badly bleached, bleary-eyed, dead-rat-for-a-moustache, chain-smoking, council estate boozer, with a profound hatred of Manchester City and further education, and a profound love for his on-off girlfriend Julie, late-night kebabs and Hofmeister lager.

Paul Calf was an immediately recognizable archetype. One only had to spend a few hours in Manchester to see people like Calf wandering around in cheap chain-store clothes hunting for bargains in the Arndale Centre. He could have been the Northern answer to Harry Enfield's Loadsamoney, except that Enfield had already done that with the skint Geordie, Buggerallmoney. He was an unreconstructed lad, not sophisticated enough to read *Loaded* perhaps, just part of a growing constituency who had little truck with being right-on

Coogan had had his own encounters with genuine Calfs when he was studying drama at Manchester Polytechnic. Born in Middleton in Manchester in 1965, he had originally applied to RADA, but failed to get in so opted for more familiar territory. These real-life loafers would hang around in the pub opposite the college or wander into the Poly bar on a Friday night in search of cheap ale and a fight, or a 'leathering' as it was known in the local vernacular. Calf was a street philosopher with his own bizarre moral code: 'Is it a crime to hit a student across the back of the head with a snooker ball in a sock?'

During a Radio 4 interview in 2001, Coogan shed some more light on how he gave birth to Calf. He likes to work from the outside in, he explained. Once he had the costume the personality would follow: 'When I first did Paul Calf, I remember getting the wig and the clothes and standing in front of a mirror and talking to myself. If I looked different, I could submerge myself in the character.' Once he had the look he didn't have to stretch himself too far to come up with a catch-all catchphrase – 'bag o' shite'.

Calf had been cropping up on late night television for a while in the early nineties, but not enough people were watching shows such as *Paramount City* and *London Underground* for him to make a splash. But he quickly hit the big time in 1993, when Coogan became part of Channel 4's *Saturday Zoo*, Jonathan Ross' short-lived attempt to twin the post-modern chat show frenzy of his breakthrough show *The Last Resort* with the booming offbeat comedy scene.

The show was not a big hit, but in retrospect Ross was certainly good at talent-spotting. Others in his rep company included Simon Day, of the *Fast Show,* and Graham Fellows, who, in the guise of Sheffield MOR song-smith John Shuttleworth briefly shared the screen with *Deer Hunter* star Christopher Walken, which is not something you see every day.

Another regular was Patrick Marber, who had been something of a mentor to the reborn, reinvented NME-friendly Coogan, directing his Perrier-winning show. A few years later ex-stand-up Marber would write the acclaimed play *Closer,* and would have to get used to being called the Harold Pinter of his generation (curious fact: this is not bad for someone whom in the late eighties I saw heckled from a stage in East Dulwich for playing a toy plastic trumpet and pretending to be a cooler-than-thou jazz musician known as 'the ice-cream man').

It was a busy, productive period for Coogan and Marber. While they were working with Ross they also had various other irons in the broadcasting fire. Coogan's appearances as Partridge on Radio 4's satirical news-spoof *On the Hour* would spawn the radio spin-off *Knowing Me, Knowing You* in 1992, and subsequently the television incarnation. The sports anchor would also appear on the magnificently-realized television version of *On the Hour, The Day Today*. These hits would conspire to make Partridge – in colleague Armando Iannucci's words, 'a sports reporter who sounds like all the sports reporters you've ever heard' – the enduring monster he is today. But that's another branch of the Coogan family tree altogether.

Saturday Zoo made Coogan's lager-fuelled lout a national talking point and a subject for critical debate. While some broadsheet snobs dissected the culture-hating Calf and saw class-hatred in place of a heart, Coogan had more sympathy for this kind of figure than first met the eye. He was the classic intelligent sixties child caught between two cultures – brought up in a large upper-working class Catholic family on a council estate, he had gone to grammar school. But he never quite left his roots behind. When there were disputes at drama college, he often found himself siding with the people from the housing estate, who had contempt for the arty farties over the road. Paul Calf's gags at the expense of artistic pretension echoed Coogan's own populist feelings on the subject: 'I pay taxes to let them pretend to be trees …'

Calf was such a hit an emboldened Coogan decided to introduce his stiletto-heeled strumpet of a sister, Pauline, to the *Saturday Zoo* audience. He had originally been thinking about playing his on-off girlfriend Julie, but decided the sister would make more sense – it would certainly explain the resemblance. Apart from the looks department, however, they were poles apart. While Pauline couldn't get enough sex ('Tits first, I'm not a slag'), Paul couldn't get any, which was not surprising, given his way with the ladies: 'Look, I'm not messing about, if you want a shag I'll be in the cubicle. Leave it about twenty minutes, I'll be having a dump.'

The success of Paul Calf's stand-up appearances prompted Coogan to open out the character: on 1 January 1994 he appeared on BBC2 in *The Paul Calf Video Diary*, co-written by comedian Henry Normal and Patrick Marber. This hilarious 'mockumentary' played on the growing trend for ordinary people to film their ordinary lives with lightweight cameras for public viewing, resulting in a mixture social history and curtain-twitching voyeurism. In Calf's case, this meant that we saw the intimate moments that we might rather have not seen. The action opened with the pasty-bodied Calf/Coogan in his bedroom and in his pants hunting for clean, or at least not too dirty, undercrackers. He was still living at home with his mother and sister Pauline and we were told that his father had died. He was advised to wear his late parent's Y-fronts, prompting the memorably defiant declaration: 'I'm not wearing dead man's pants.'

The action was shot in Eccles, 20 minutes by car from Coogan's Middleton roots. I remember doing a location report, and during filming Henry Normal offered me the chance to be an extra in a fancy dress party scene. Unfortunately, I had to get back to London. My lasting memory is of Coogan strutting his stuff as Calf and Fat Bob (John Thomson) walking past me carrying the video camera and painted green. Throughout the film you only saw his green arm, but at the end it turned out that he had come to the party as the Incredible Hulk.

At the end of the same year, there was a second instalment of life with the Calf clan, the BAFTA-winning sequel entitled *Three Fights, Two Weddings and a Funeral*. This time the focus was more on Pauline, who was about to tie the knot with new boyfriend Spiros. In the end though, she takes a leaf out of Hugh Grant's book and jilts him for Paul's long-suffering car mechanic sidekick, Fat Bob.

Comedians are always asked where they get their material from, and in this case, for a change, we have a straight answer. In 2001, Coogan confessed that they came up with the title first (as a parody of the then recent hit movie *Four*

Weddings and a Funeral); he then came up with a plot to fit the title. They even managed to secure the services of John Hannah who had a cameo sending up his role in the box office-busting romantic comedy.

Paul Calf helped to establish Coogan as a major comedy star. His facility for becoming fictional creations was drawing favourable comparisons with Peter Sellers – Coogan didn't shy away from them, he just said that he hoped he lived longer than Sellers. And as with many great stars, he was ahead of the game. By the mid-nineties, character comedy was coming back into vogue and edging out traditional stand-up. There was already the aforementioned John Shuttleworth and now Al Murray was nurturing his embryonic Pub Landlord and Rich Hall was thinking about a Tennessee jailbird called Otis Lee Crenshaw. As for *The League of Gentlemen*, they had a whole village up their tuxedoed sleeves.

Coogan was given the chance to showcase his own comic menagerie in a six-part series, *Coogan's Run*, set in the fictional outpost of Ottle, in which he played a different character each week. The highlight was hapless software salesman Gareth Cheeseman (a clear, if unwitting forerunner of David Brent), who appeared in an episode written by Father Ted creators Graham Linehan and Arthur Mathews. Calf was also present and correct in *Get Calf*. This time around he was accidentally involved in an armed robbery and pursued by real villains. Pauline and Fat Bob now had a little daughter called Petula, but Paul was still an unemployed waster. Some things never changed.

The days were numbered for this icon of sloth. He was an effective character to trundle out for live shows, as the routine featured here recorded at a 1994 Aids benefit amply demonstrates. If Partridge was more psychologically and linguistically complex, Calf was a great vessel for simple, lewd gags: 'I've given up two of my worst habits: smoking and masturbation. 'Cos I'm a twenty a day man, and I smoke like a chimney.'

Which is not to say he has smoked his last fag or hurled his last insult at a passing undergraduate. In 2003, the BBC aired Paul and Pauline Calf's *Cheese and Ham Sandwich*, a live show filmed at Liverpool's Neptune Theatre. A decade on from *Saturday Zoo*, it was nice to know that something hadn't changed. Calf was still a human distillery: 'I'm on disability benefit,' he explained. 'I sometimes can't walk. Normally at the end of lunchtime and late in the evening.' If Coogan decided to bring him back again he could easily reposition him as the original king of the chavs.

But as the nineties drew to a close, he had other things on his mind. In 1997 there was an all-new creation, crooner Tony Ferrino, who didn't quite set the world alight. When he chose to fall back on old favourites, Alan Partridge seemed to have more potential. Calf was still stuck at home with his mum, but as Partridge's career went into freefall, the scope for the comedy of embarrassment was endless. Anyone for monkey tennis?

In 2006 Coogan continued to pursue the holy grail of the perfect sitcom, creating *Saxondale*, about a pot-bellied ex-roadie-turned-pest controller in Stevenage.

Coogan also had an eye on the big screen and, by 2001, after frequent supporting roles, was big enough to play the lead in *The Parole Officer*. This was the first in a sequence of films that were wildly variable in terms of quality. Yet even the bad films have shown what a versatile performer Coogan is.

If *The Parole Officer* was positively criminal, he had better luck playing Factory Records mogul Tony Wilson in Michael Winterbottom's glittering portrait of the Manchester music scene, *24 Hour Party People*. It was a remarkable spot-on performance portraying the legendary maverick as half-twat, half-genius. And if critics said that he played Wilson as if he was a close relation of Alan Partridge, there was a reason for that. Coogan had known Wilson for many years and when he created Partridge he had intentionally put a bit of Wilson's misfiring arrogance in there. The wheel had, in effect, come right round.

24 Hour Party People was seen by industry people in Hollywood and opened up more doors for Coogan. Unfortunately, he walked straight into the dreary remake of *Around the World in 80 Days* alongside Jackie Chan. Michael Winterbottom came to the rescue again though, with the breathtakingly funny part-period adaptation, *A Cock and Bull Story*, in which Coogan played Tristram Shandy, Tristram Shandy's father and an actor called Steve Coogan. The behind-the-scenes banter with Rob Brydon contains some of the finest comedy moments Coogan has ever committed to film. The petty rivalries, jealousies and status games also give the viewer a remarkable insight into the nature of celebrity.

Anyone who saw the focused, determined young man at the Edinburgh Festival in 1992 knew it was only a matter of time before Coogan would be a success on both the small screen and the big screen. What has been more of a surprise is that he has been a success behind the screen too. In 2001, he formed an independent television production company with Henry Normal to nurture new names. They have picked up on some terrific talent in recent years, giving Rob Brydon his first television break in *Marion & Geoff*, allowing Julia Davis to get very dark in *Nighty Night*, and making cult stars out of Julian Barratt and Noel Fielding in BBC2's *The Mighty Boosh*.

The name of his company suggests that there is one character that he has a real soft spot for. He didn't call it Partridge Productions or Pear Tree Programmes. He called it Baby Cow. Paul Calf might be gone, but to those that love comedy enough to sit through the credits, his name lives on.

Bruce Dessau

'Paul Calf'

Recorded for the Terrence Higgins Trust,
Sadlers Wells Theatre, London (1994),
Laughing Stock LAFFCD 0175

Hey, hey, do you know what? I think it's great, this. I think it's very good, like, tonight, you know Terrence Higgins Trust, because I … I'm … I'm not prejudiced. I'm not … I'm not prejudiced, right?

I don't care who you are, right? You could be gay, straight, bisexual, homosexual, black, white. I don't care who you are, you know? If you give me grief you get a bit of that, right?

[*Laughter*]

You know and I'm not scared to talk about sex. I … I … I'll say it … cunnilingus.

[*Laughter*]

I … I'll fucking shout it, cunnilingus, yeah? Totally fucking amazing is what I'm saying.

[*Laughter*]

I know … I know, you know, it's not how women are on the outside, because that's not important, you know? It's how they are on the inside that matters, how … how they are as a human being and their personality, you know? And if they've got big tits, that's a bonus …

[*Laughter*]

Yeah, but you've got to be very careful
when you … when you bring them back to your
house, like, because … because if you're
both pissed you've got to … you've got to
be careful. So what I do is I get them to
sign a contract, a sexual contract. This is
what she has to sign, right, if she's going
to have sex with me, [*Snorting*] right?

I, being of sound mind and … and not a bad
body, right, agree to have a shag with Mr
Paul Calf, right, on his settee/back of
car, right, on me back, on top and doggie
and … and any other positions to be
mutually agreed, right?

[*Laughter*]

And this is the good bit, right? In the
small print I put here, I also agree,
right, that when Paul has come/passed out,
to sleep on the wet patch.

[*Laughter*]

But, hey, a quick … a word … word for the
lads, right? Seduction, right, it … it …
it's an art form, right? You can't just
say, 'Hello, darling, fancy a shag?' You
know what I mean? You got to say please.

[*Laughter*]

You got to sweet talk them, you know?
'Hello, what's your name? My name's Paul.
Do you fancy a shag, *please*?'

[*Laughter*]

You know what I mean, you know what I mean? You've got to be sophisticated. [*Snorting*] And don't, for fuck's sake, don't forget their name. Don't forget their name. Write it down if you have to.

[*Laughter*]

On their back if need be.

[*Laughter*]

I always keep a felt-tipped pen by the bed, you know, just in case. [*Snorting*]

But you know … you know, talk to them, talk … while you're having sex, talk to each other, you know, you know? And be polite. Say, you know, 'Would you tickle my balls, please,' you know?

[*Laughter*]

'Would you like me to suck your tits?' Start a dialogue. Do you know what I mean? [*Snorting*]

But I'm … I'm still missing me girlfriend, Julie. She … she… she's pissed off, but I've written her this letter to try and get her back, right? See if you reckon this'll do the trick, [*Snorting*] right? So I'll read the letter to her, right?

'Dear Julie … I can't stop thinking about you. We had some good times and some bad times. Remember when I was sick in the back of that taxi and he … [*Laughter*] and he threw us out in the middle of the Peak district at two o'clock in the morning in the pouring rain and all we had was half a can of lager.' [*Burping*]

'And … and there were bad times as well …'

[*Laughter*]

'Like when we didn't have any lager at all.'

[*Laughter*]

'Yesterday I found your boob tube in the boot of the Cortina. I remember the last time you wore it. It was that night I was set upon by five students and I fucking leathered the lot of them. Why can't it always be like that?'

[*Laughter*]

'I'll never forget that look on your face that night. Shagging in the back of my car …'

'I wish it had been me.'

[*Laughter, applause*]

'I … I want you to know I will change. I … I'll try and give up two of me worst habits, smoking and masturbation, which I'm finding difficult as I'm a 20 a day man and I smoke like a chimney.'

[*Laughter*]

Hey, hey, I remember the last time I had sex with Julie. Oh, it … I was about to come, right. I was right … right on coming. She said, 'No, Paul, don't come, don't, don't. Think of *Esther Rantzen* …'

I shot me fucking load.

[*Laughter*]

Still … still, that's life, hey?

[*Laughter*, *applause*]

Thanks very much. You've been lovely. Goodnight.

[*Applause*]

'Pauline Calf'

Recorded for the Terrence Higgins Trust,
Sadlers Wells Theatre, London (1994),
Laughing Stock LAFFCD 0175

Hi there, you alright?

Nice that Mark Lamarr, isn't he?

I've had 'im.

[*Laughter*]

Hey, listen, I've got something to tell you
… I'm pregnant.

Don't ask me who the father is, 'cos I
don't know …

[*Laughter*]

No, no, I'll give you a clue, I'll give you
a clue.

Um, right, his jackets are designed by
Jean-Michel Jarre and his shirts, they're
by Fettuccini, and he wears Kevin Kline's
underpants. Can you tell?

It's Jonathan Ross. Yeah. Yeah, he's
lovely, Jonathan. He's got class, like me.

Class is like the clap — you've either got
it or you haven't.

[*Laughter*].

I've got it, and so has Jonathan.

[*Laughter*].

Hey, but listen, lads, if you're trying to seduce a woman, right, just a couple of tips, right. If you take them back to your place, you know, be sophisticated, right, you know.

Sort of like, you know, put a bit of light music on. The Carpenters — something like that.

[*Laughter*].

Lower the lights, you know. Take your socks off. You know, little things like that … makes all the difference. If you nip into the toilet, you know, while you're in there, rinse your knob out in the sink.

[*Applause*]

You know, a clean penis might just tip the balance.

[*Laughter*]

Oh, and, ah, God, do you know what, I think is absolutely gorgeous? I think he's fucking gorgeous — Patrick Swayze. I've seen *Dirty Dancing* 25 times. Oh, it's fanta— There's a bloke round our way is just like Patrick Swayze, yeah. Wears an orthopaedic shoe, works in John Menzies.

[*Laughter*]

Oh, honest to God, he's lovely. He's really nice. Very imaginative lover, you know, it's really … he'll give me a choice, you know, he'll say, you know, Pauline, you know, do you want us to make love to ya, you know, or do you just want to suck us off … Do you know what I mean? Variety! You know.

Hey, but you know our Paul? Listen, you know who's a real model for you, a real gentleman, is my brother Barry Calf, but don't tell Paul I mentioned Barry right … 'Cos he'll go spare, honest to God.

What happened to our Barry, it's terrible, he was a lovely lad, but he got in trouble with the police now and again, well he was a fucking head case you know, made our Paul look like Gandhi right.

But ah, but to cut a long story short, he got banged up for attempted murder right, and what happens in prison right he starts mixing with the wrong sort of people right … ten years later he's got an Open University degree in criminology, lecturing at Warwick University …

[*Laughter*]

He knows that John McVicar.

I've had 'im

I showed him some criminal activities …

Do you what I can't fucking stand?

Sinead O'Connor.

Honest, she's a miserable cow, isn't she? I reckon they should get her on *Generation Game*, you know. And then they could say, come on, Sinead, give us a twirl. She'll go, no, I don't want to.

And hey, Sinead O'Connor, eh, nothing
compares to you …

Kojak does, don't he ? Hey? Hey?

I've had 'im.

Yeah. I was on top.

I said, 'Hey, look everyone, I'm on Telly.'

[*Laughter and applause*].

6. PETE & DUD

I've got nothing against your right leg …

I met Peter Cook twice. The first time was in the summer of 1982, when I was working as a dustman in Hampstead, and he was living in Perrin's Walk, a quiet, attractive mews round the back of the Everyman cinema. Every Thursday we would clear the bins from outside his small, flat-fronted house. I've not got many regrets in life, but one of them is that I didn't rummage through his rubbish. I never really was very good at learning about people from what they throw out, although I did once notice a bottle of Silvikrin shampoo in the bin of flaxen-haired former Labour party leader Michael Foot.

I didn't ever see Cook hanging around by his door, but one sunny morning we were doing the row of shops on Hampstead High Street and I spotted him walking down the road. It was about eight o'clock and he somehow managed to look both attractively louche and horribly dishevelled. I wished him well and he vaguely smiled back at me. He might have been nipping out for a paper but it looked more like he was returning home after an extremely late night out.

By this time Peter Cook had been a legend for so long it was hard to pinpoint one particular thing that made him so famous. Historically speaking, it could have been his role in ushering in the satire boom when Beyond the Fringe opened in London in 1961. Beyond the Fringe was comedy's answer to the theatre's Angry Young Men, debunking the old order and demanding a change. While plenty of their material did not attack sacred cows, it was the stabs at the state of post-War Britain that made a real dent on the British psyche.

Cook's impersonation of then prime minister Harold Macmillan ('There are many people in this country today who are far worse off than yourself. And it is the policy of the Conservative Party to see that this position is maintained.') was the height of daring and touched a nerve. The Conservative Party had been in power for a decade, and Cook, in particular, tapped into a feeling that perhaps their time was up.

Macmillan once said 'You've never had it so good,' yet by the early sixties there was definitely a mood that the country was divided into the haves and have-nots. The Beyond the Fringe team – Cook, Dudley Moore, Alan Bennett and Jonathan Miller – exploited this rift in the nation, and made their names. As Cook wrote himself 'I never had it so good. I had a flat in Battersea, a Hillman Convertible and the chance to show off every night.'

Cook has other claims to fame too. He is also known for founding The Establishment Club – he had seen cabaret nights in France and Germany in the late fifties, and was terrified that someone would do it here before he had the chance. But they didn't, and he opened the Establishment in Greek Street in 1961. The cream of the British satire boom – John Bird, John Fortune, Eleanor Bron – appeared there alongside performers ranging from Lenny Bruce to Frankie Howerd (curious fact: once Bruce wanted Cook to score some heroin for him – Cook asked Dudley Moore, but the strongest drug Dudley could get his hands on at short notice was soluble Aspirin).

He could be remembered for his support – financial and intellectual – of *Private Eye*. He did not launch the irreverent magazine, but came up with the idea of the spoof news-paper headline front covers, and bailed them out when they had money problems. He was the kind of proprietor every publication dreams of – he never censored or edited the magazine, but was great company at lunch and occasionally swished into the office and came up with an exceptionally witty line.

But for many it was his long on-off partnership with Dudley Moore that secured his fame – and notably his place in the comedy pantheon. Peter Cook and Dudley Moore were a double act par excellence, with an instinctive (almost telepathic) rapport to die for. Cook was the tall, middle-class Cambridge graduate and ex-public schoolboy from Torquay; Moore was the short, working-class Oxford graduate with the club foot from Dagenham.

They were, however, the double act that was not a double act. Cook and Moore first met in 1960 when they were put together with Alan Bennett and Jonathan Miller by the assistant to the director of the Edinburgh Festival, John Bassett. He wanted a new alternative late-night revue and called it Beyond the Fringe. If the groundbreaking format, made up of bits of existing material with some new sketches added on, had not been a success the quartet would have probably gone their separate ways. But instead the show transferred to London in 1961, and then to New York, where it was the talk of the town.

The duo took part in two sketches that, along with the audacious Macmillan monologue, confirmed the quartet's satirical reputation for saying the unsayable. The foursome's 'Civil War' skit mocked government plans for a nuclear attack by suggesting people jump into brown paper bags to avoid radiation. Meanwhile 'Aftermyth of War' famously sent up the stiff upper lips and class-riddled idiocy of the British military as portrayed in World War II films: 'I want you to lay down your life Perkins. We need a futile gesture at this stage. It will raise the whole tone of the war.'

Despite the acclaim of the Broadway critics, Cook and Moore were still set on going their separate ways after the show. In 1964, Moore had been offered a one-off BBC show and he decided to get Cook in as a guest rather than a partner.

Cook's pieces included the instantly successful, gloomy, raincoat-wearing bore, who droned on at length about nothing in particular but was incredibly funny. This character was instantly recognizable as E.L. Wisty, even though the name was not used because Cook had used it in a previous ITV show. When the BBC decided to turn the show into a series Cook took on a more permanent role. The result was *Not Only … But Also*, which first aired in January 1965.

The show was remarkable for its consistently high number of hits. As well as Wisty, there was Cook's bumptious duffer Arthur Streeb-Greebling, who waxed lyrical about his new restaurant, The Frog and Peach, where you could get anything to eat as long as it contained frog. Or peach. Spawn cocktail was a *specialité de la maison*. Then there was a revival of Cook's old pre-Beyond the Fringe skit 'One Leg Too Few', in which he played a theatrical producer and Moore played a man with one leg auditioning for the part of Tarzan: 'I've got nothing against your right leg. The trouble is – neither have you.'

Their brilliant bantering style had a huge influence on future comedians. Their dreamy, flat-capped, beer-sipping 'Dagenham Dialogues', about everything, from kicking Greta Garbo out of the bedroom, to modern art, to trying fly to the moon on gossamer wings, was a direct inspiration for the head-to-head chin-wags of Mel Smith and Griff Rhys Jones two decades later. Cook took great delight in making Moore corpse, improvising wildly and shooting off on absurd tangents just to get the desired effect.

'The Psychiatrist' sketch, featured here, perfectly encapsulates the winning Cook/Moore dynamic and lays bare the politeness and reserve of the English middle class professional. Cook plays the consummately unflappable shrink Dr Braintree, Moore plays nervy, neurotic patient Roger, who has been having therapy so that he can be more confident with women (not that Moore needed this sort of assistance in reality – he was married four times).

Dr Braintree's sessions have been so successful Roger has met and fallen in love with a woman, only this woman happens to be Dr Braintree's wife. And so that they can be together, Roger says he is going to have to kill Dr Braintree. Of course, he can't do it now, he will have to make an appointment. Will next Wednesday do, enquires Dr Braintree? 'If you could pop along at 9.30 and kill me then …'

The other sketch featured here, 'A Bit of a Chat', also nails what it is to be English, uptight and repressed, this time dealing more directly with sex. Cook plays the father who fumblingly attempts to explain to his son (Moore) how he was conceived – 'the method whereby you came to be brought about' – but cannot bring himself to be more graphic than to suggest that she sat on a chair that he had recently vacated and thus was still warm from his body – 'and sure enough, four years later you were born.'

Not Only … But Also was a huge mainstream hit for the duo and inevitably opened more doors. Cinema was the natural next step, and in 1966 they co-starred in *The Wrong Box*, the story of a Victorian inheritance squabble based on a Robert Louis Stevenson story. In 1967, they made *Bedazzled*, a swinging contemporary spin on the Faust legend, with Cook as the devil and Moore as short order burger flipper Stanley Moon. In 1969, they appeared in the all-star car-chase caper *Monte Carlo or Bust*. All the films had their moments – Stanley Moon getting his wish to be a fly on the wall and getting swatted was a great gag – but none quite captured the magic of their television work.

Even so, the films fared better than Cook's stab at presenting a chat show in 1971. *Where Do I Sit?* had the ignominy of being pulled from the schedules after three episodes. It was ironic that Cook, a great talker who could improvise at length, found himself struggling when he finally had a whole live show to himself. Welcoming Hollywood's Kirk Douglas on stage Cook meant to say, 'How are you?', but nerves and possibly alcohol got the better of him and he blurted out 'Who are you?'

As the years passed cracks began to appear in the Cook/Moore relationship. There was always an unspoken power struggle between them, born out of a cocktail of rivalry, jealousy, competitiveness and ambition. The situation was further compounded by Cook's increasingly heavy drinking.

They were destined to appear together again, however – although whether they intended it to be for public consumption or not is debatable to this day. In 1973, they went into a studio and did a freeform foulmouthed variant of Pete & Dud, pushing things as far as possible and seeing how rude, crude and shocking they could really get, discussing cancer, masturbation, and doing unspeakable things with lobsters and Jayne Mansfield. Somehow bootlegs of these new alter egos, Derek & Clive, began to circulate, first in the music industry, and then among eager teenagers with tape recorders and friends in low places.

When the taboo-busting tapes were officially released as *Derek and Clive Live*, *Come Again* and *Ad Nauseam* in the late seventies, they chimed nicely with the subversive punk mood of the day. Anything the Sex Pistols could do, Pete & Dud could do with knobs on. *Ad Nauseam* even answered the critics who said it was unpalatable by coming complete with a sick bag for disgusted listeners to vomit into.

Derek & Clive would, however, be the last time Cook and Moore produced anything new of lasting value together. In 1978, they co-starred in a bizarre remake of *The Hound of the Baskervilles*, which is only really notable for a scene in which a dog urinates excessively. By the late seventies, Moore had decided to try his luck in Hollywood and when George Segal dropped out of Blake Edwards' romantic comedy *10*, Moore stepped in and became an unlikely sex symbol.

Cook meanwhile stayed mainly in Britain, intermittently offering flashes of what he could truly be capable of if only he would drink less and work harder. In 1978, he played the malevolent compere on television pop show *Revolver*; in 1979, he did a turn as an exquisitely prejudiced judge in the 'The Secret Policeman's Ball'.

Separately, however, there were few moments that matched the brilliance of their early work together. Moore's movies ranged from the moderate to the mediocre, while Cook drifted from project to project and made a fair number of dubious big screen appearances himself in films such as *Supergirl* and *Yellowbeard*. The only consistently interesting aspect to Cook's work in the eighties was the way he was taken on as a talisman by younger comics. He had a cameo as Richard III in the first episode of *The Black Adder* (Atkinson had guested in Cook's patchy 1980 ITV show *Peter Cook & Co*), he appeared with Alexei Sayle in the Dr Strangelove-ish *Whoops Apocalypse* and as a serial killer with the rest of the Comic Strip team in *Mr Jolly Lives Next Door*. In 1989, however, the duo reunited at the latest Amnesty gala and revisited their 'One Leg Too Few' classic in front of a new generation of fans.

The second time I met Cook it was in the early nineties. The movie *Derek and Clive Get the Horn* had just been re-issued on video, and he agreed to be interviewed to plug it. We met in the Everyman Cinema's cafe by his house. It was very early in the day, but this time I'm sure Cook had been to bed. In fact, I think he still had his slippers on. He was looking less louche but just as dishevelled. I know it was morning because Cook ordered a fried breakfast. He also ordered a Bloody Mary.

We settled into the interview and disaster promptly struck when my tape recorder ground to a halt. Rather than be imperious and annoyed as I might have expected, Cook was considerate and immediately came up with a suggestion – we went back to his house to borrow a tape recorder.

On arrival, he disappeared upstairs, offering me the opportunity for a Loyd Grossman-style *Through the Keyhole* nose around. What sort of a comedy icon lives here? Golf clubs leaned against one wall – Cook was a surprisingly useful golfer. On the sofa and table there were piles of newspapers and magazines. He was a voracious reader. A large television dominated the room, a reminder that when not phoning local radio phone-in shows pretending to be a lovelorn Scandinavian fisherman called Sven, Cook would spend late nights watching bizarre low-budget foreign game shows and no-budget talk shows.

Eventually Cook returned. Not with a Sony Walkman as I expected, but with a huge suitcase-sized ghetto blaster. We then trudged over to the local electrical shop to buy some batteries and a tape. I think Cook kindly paid or at least I hope he did, because I didn't. It was a great interview, however, most significant for the fact that he kept insisting that Johnny Rotten had stolen his droll, deadpan delivery.

It is a tragedy that when Peter Cook died he was on the verge of another burst of creativity. In 1993, Radio 3 broadcast a series of improvised chats between Chris Morris and Peter Cook in the guise of Arthur Streeb-Greebling entitled *Why Bother?* This seemed to re-energize Cook, who then appeared on a special edition of Channel 4 chat show *Clive Anderson Talks Back* playing all of the guests. Most vivid was Cook's obsessive northern football manager Alan Latchley, who talked enthusiastically about soccer in a series of meaningless sayings, such as 'Motivation, motivation, motivation – the three Ms.'

Old people know where they were when they heard that JFK had been shot; young people know where they were when they heard about 9/11. I'm in the middle, but I certainly remember where I was on 9 January 1995, when I heard that Peter Cook had died. I was driving up the M6 on the way to Manchester to interview Caroline Aherne. The news stuck in my mind because at the time Aherne was married to Peter Hook of New Order and I thought for a moment Radio 4 was announcing that it was Peter Hook who had died, aged 57, in the Royal Free Hospital as a result of a gastrointestinal haemorrhage.

Dudley Moore attended Cook's memorial service, but was soon to be diagnosed with progressive supranuclear palsy.

He died, aged 66, on 27 March 2002. Together this unique duo left behind a body of work that paved the way for pretty much any type of comedy that came after them.

Would we have had Monty Python without the irreverent ambition of Beyond the Fringe? I doubt it. Would we have had Fry and Laurie, without Cook and Moore? Probably, but they might have struggled to break into the mainstream. Would we have had *Have I Got News For You?* without Cook's satirical agenda-setting? Definitely not. Modern comedy would simply not be modern comedy without them.

Bruce Dessau

'The Psychiatrist'

Recorded for *Not Only … But Also* (1965),
Laughing Stock LAFFCD 110

DR BRAINTREE, PLAYED BY PETER COOK

ROGER, PLAYED BY DUDLEY MOORE

[*Knocking*]

DR BRAINTREE

Come in.

[*Door opening*]

DR BRAINTREE

Hello, Roger.

ROGER

Hello, Dr Braintree.

DR BRAINTREE

Hello, come in.

ROGER

I'm so sorry I'm late.

DR BRAINTREE

That's quite all right.

ROGER

Yes.

DR BRAINTREE

How are you?

ROGER

  I'm very well, thank you.

DR BRAINTREE

  Would you like to sit down or would you
  prefer to lie?

ROGER

  I'll sit, thank you.

  [*Laughter*]

DR BRAINTREE

  Right, well, sit right down. Now, tell me,
  how are you in yourself?

ROGER

  Well, I'm … I'm really feeling rather in
  the pink.

DR BRAINTREE

  Oh, this is terrific.

ROGER

  Yes. It's funny, really, you know? If
  anybody had told me that talking to a
  psychiatrist would've helped me at all, I'd
  have laughed in their faces, you know?

DR BRAINTREE

  Yes.

ROGER

  But I can honestly say that our little
  chats together have … have really been of
  tremendous benefit to me.

113

DR BRAINTREE

I'm so glad, Roger. Of course, a lot of
people are instinctively very suspicious of
psychiatry and possibly, you know, with
reason, but it can help in times.

ROGER

Well, I … I really think it can, because,
you know, I've got so much more self-
confidence now.

DR BRAINTREE

Yes, yes, yes.

ROGER

And I'm … I'm … I'm much less self-
conscious in the company of the opposite
sex, which I wasn't, as you know.
[*Laughing*]

DR BRAINTREE

You're less inhibited, are you?

ROGER

Oh, I should say so…

[*Laughter*]

DR BRAINTREE

Good. This is terrific.

ROGER

And the wonderful thing is, really, about
it all, is well, I'm … I'm in love.

DR BRAINTREE

Oh, this is wonderful news, Roger. You're
in love. With a woman?

ROGER

Yes.

DR BRAINTREE

Oh, so much …

[*Laughter*]

DR BRAINTREE

So much the better. That's terrific.

ROGER

You know, it's so wonderful to be in love.
I can't tell you the … the absolute joy I
have.

DR BRAINTREE

Well, love is a wonderful thing. I've been
there myself. It's a wonderful thing.

[*Laughter*]

ROGER

I mean, she's … this girl … this … this
creature … this goddess…

DR BRAINTREE

Yes.

ROGER

It's so … you know, it's so right.

DR BRAINTREE

Yes, yes.

ROGER

Everything is so wonderful, you know?

DR BRAINTREE

Yes, yes, yes, you really … you really click together?

ROGER

Yes. [*Laughter*] Oh, it's … it's so marvellous, but the only trouble is that apart from this wonderful light-hearted love that I have, I …

DR BRAINTREE

Yes, yes.

ROGER

I seem to be saddled with this tremendous burning sense of guilt.

DR BRAINTREE

You have guilt as well as love? Well, this is … this is … this is unfortunate, Roger. You know, sex is the most natural healthy thing in the world. There's no reason at all to have any guilt about it. I mean, why would you have guilt about sex? It's a lovely, beautiful thing, Roger.

ROGER

Well, it's … it's not really as simple as that, you know? It's … it's rather

116

difficult to explain. I … I don't really
know where to start.

DR BRAINTREE

Well, begin at the beginning. [*Laughter*]
That's always the best, you know. What's
the girl's name?

ROGER

Stephanie.

DR BRAINTREE

Stephanie? That's a lovely name, isn't it?
Well, my wife's name, in fact, isn't it?

[*Laughter*]

ROGER

Yes. [*Laughter*] It's … it's Stephanie.

DR BRAINTREE

Yes. It's Stephanie.

ROGER

No. It's Stephanie.

DR BRAINTREE

Yes. It's Stephanie, Roger.

ROGER

Yes. It's … it's Stephanie. It's your wife,
Stephanie.

DR BRAINTREE

Oh, you're in love with my wife, Stephanie?

ROGER

Yes.

DR BRAINTREE

Well, this is a perfectly understandable
thing, Roger. She's a very attractive
woman. I married her myself. I don't see
why you should feel upset about that.

ROGER

But she's in love with me.

DR BRAINTREE

Well, this again is perfectly
understandable, Roger. I mean, you're a
perfectly attractive human being, as I've
told you over the last few weeks. There's
nothing repulsive about you, is there?
There's no reason why a highly sexed woman
such as Stephanie shouldn't fall in love
with you, and I must explain to you, Roger,
that I'm a very busy man. I have many, many
patients to see. [*Laughter*] I see rather
less of my wife perhaps than I should, and
I think it's very understandable that she
should seek some sort of companionship
outside the marriage. I don't think that's
unreasonable at all.

ROGER

But she's not … she's not seeking anything
outside marriage, Dr Braintree, and nor am
I. We want to get married.

118

DR BRAINTREE

Well, this, again, I think is perfectly … [*Laughter*] perfectly understandable. After all, you're two young people in love. You want to manifest your love feelings within the confines of a bourgeois society through marriage. I think this is very appropriate.

ROGER

The awful thing is, you see, I should feel so grateful to you for what you've done for me and … and all I can feel is this … this burning jealousy. I can't bear the thought of you touching her.

DR BRAINTREE

Well, of course you can't. I can understand it. [*Laughter*] One is tremendously possessive about someone one loves. One is tremendously possessive. It would be unhealthy not to have this jealous reaction, Roger.

ROGER

But don't you see? I … I hate you for it.

DR BRAINTREE

Of course you hate me, Roger.

ROGER

I hate you for being so near her.

DR BRAINTREE

Yes. Of course you hate me, Roger. You love to hate the one who loves the one you hate

to love the one you hate. [*Laughter*] This
is a very old rule, Roger. There's nothing
to feel ashamed about. It's absolutely
reasonable.

ROGER

Don't you understand? I … I want to kill
you.

DR BRAINTREE

Of course you want to kill me, because by
killing me, Roger, you eradicate the one
you hate. This is a perfectly natural
reaction, Roger.

ROGER

You're so reasonable, aren't you?

DR BRAINTREE

Yes. I am.

ROGER

You understand it all so much. You're so
logical.

DR BRAINTREE

Yes. I am. It's my job, Roger.

ROGER

I'm going to have to kill you now.

DR BRAINTREE

Ah, Roger, this is a little inconvenient
[*Laughter*] because I have another patient
at 6:30 and then there's somebody else at
7:00 after that. I wonder if you could make

it some time next week? [*Laughter*] Could
you make it earlier in the week, say?

ROGER

When ... when do you think?

DR BRAINTREE

How are you ... [*Laughter*] how are you fixed
on Wednesday morning? Say at 9:30, would
that be convenient?

ROGER

Oh, yes, that's perfect.

DR BRAINTREE

Right. Well, if you could pop along at 9:30
and kill me then?

[*Laughter*]

ROGER

Once again, Dr Braintree, I'm ... I'm amazed,
you know, really, I'm so grateful to you
for, you know, for showing me the way.

DR BRAINTREE

It's what I'm here for, Roger.

ROGER

Thank you so much.

DR BRAINTREE

Thank you. And with a bit of luck this
should be the last time you need to visit
me.

[*Applause*]

'A Bit of a Chat'

Recorded for *Not Only ... But Also* (1965),
Laughing Stock LAFFCD 110

FATHER, PLAYED BY PETER COOK

ROGER, PLAYED BY DUDLEY MOORE

[*Whistling*]

FATHER

Is that you, Roger?

ROGER

Yes, father.

FATHER

A cup of tea here, boy, if you'd like one.

ROGER

That's very kind of you, sir, but I've just
come in from rugger and I'm a bit grubby. I
think I ought to go and have a shower
first, sir.

FATHER

Well, pour me a cup, there's a good chap,
would you.

ROGER

Certainly, sir. Yes, of course.

FATHER

Thank you. How was school today?

ROGER

Oh, much as usual, thank you, sir, but I, I
caught someone having a crafty smoke behind
the wooden buildings. Had to give him
rather a ticking off. Such a filthy habit,
you know, sir.

FATHER

It's a filthy habit, Roger.

ROGER

Yes. There we are, sir. Now, if you'll
excuse me.

FATHER

Thank you. Oh, Roger?

ROGER

Yes, sir.

FATHER

Um, sit down. Roger? Your mother and I were
having a bit of a chat the other day and
she thought it might be a good idea if I
was to have a bit of a chat with you.

[*Laughter*]

ROGER

Um, a bit of a chat, sir?

FATHER

A bit of a chat, yes, Roger, just a bit of
a chat.

ROGER

Um, what about, sir?

FATHER

Well, it's nothing to be worried about,
Roger, it's just that, um, well, to be
perfectly frank, how old are you?

[*Laughter*]

ROGER

Well, to be perfectly frank, sir, I'm
coming up to 18.

FATHER

Just coming up to 18.

ROGER

Well, on the verge …

FATHER

On the verge of 18. Yes. Well, I thought it
might be a good idea to have a bit of a
chat now because I remember from my own
experience that it was when I was just, you
know, coming up to 18 …

ROGER

On the verge …

FATHER

On the verge of it, that I first began to
take a serious interest in the, um, in the
opposite, um, the opposite number..

[*Laughter*]

FATHER

Now, I don't know, Roger, if you know anything about the method whereby you came to be brought about.

[*Laughter*]

ROGER

Well, sir, some of the boys at school say very filthy things about it, sir.

FATHER

This is what I was worried about, and this is why I thought I'd have a bit of a chat and explain absolutely, frankly and openly, the method whereby you, and everybody in this world, came to be.

[*Laughter*]

FATHER

Roger, in order …

[*Laughter*]

FATHER

… in order for you to be brought about, it was necessary for your mother and I to do something.

[*Laughter*]

FATHER

In particular, it was necessary for your mother … it was necessary for your mother to sit on a chair, to sit on a chair which I had recently vacated and which was still warm from my body. And then something very mysterious, rather wonderful and beautiful happened, and, sure enough, four years later, you were born. Now, there's nothing unhealthy about this, Roger. There's nothing unnatural. It's a beautiful thing in the right hands, and there's no need to think less of your mother because of it. She had to do it, she did it, and here you are.

ROGER

I must say, it's very kind of you to tell me. One thing actually slightly alarms me: I was sitting in this very chair yesterday, sir, and I vacated it, and the cat sat on it while it was still warm. Um, should we have it destroyed?

FATHER

It's a lovely chair, Roger.

ROGER

I meant the cat, sir.

FATHER

Destroyed? Oh, no, Roger, you don't understand. This thing of which I speak can only happen between two people who are married, and you are not married.

ROGER

Not yet, anyway, sir.

FATHER

Not to the cat, in any case. Well, Roger, now you have this knowledge about chairs and warmth, I hope, I hope you'll use it wisely.

ROGER

Sir.

FATHER

And take no notice of your school friends or what Uncle Bertie may say.

ROGER

Dirty Uncle Bertie, they call him.

FATHER

Dirty Uncle Bertie! And they're right, Roger. Your Uncle Bertie is a dirty, dirty man. He's been living with us now for 40 years and it does seem a day too much. You know, if it hadn't been for your mother, Roger, I'd, I don't know where we'd have been. She's the only person who can really cope with Uncle Bertie. She's the only one who can really deal with him. I don't know if you realize this, Roger, but your mother even has to sleep in the same bed as Uncle Bertie to prevent him getting up to anything in the night.

[*Laughter*]

FATHER

If only there were more people like your mother, Roger.

ROGER

Well, I'm, I'm very pleased that you've
told me this, sir, because, as I say, I'm
very glad I don't have to believe all those
filthy things that the boys at school say,
and only yesterday Uncle Bertie said to me
...

FATHER

Take no notice of Uncle Bertie, Roger. He's
a sick, sick man, and we should feel sorry
for him.

ROGER

Well, I'll try, sir. Well, thank you, sir.
Um, I wonder if I should take a cup of tea
up to mother while it's ...

FATHER

I wouldn't do that, Roger. She's upstairs
at the moment ... coping with Uncle Bertie.

[*Laughter*]

ROGER

Poor Uncle Bertie.

FATHER

Poor Uncle Bertie.

[*Applause*]

7. LENNY HENRY

Ooookaaaay!

Comedy's gain is welding's loss. It would hardly be contentious to say that Lenny Henry is a national treasure. He is respected by his peers, loved by the nation, and in 1999 was awarded the CBE in recognition of his work with Comic Relief. Which is not bad for a lad from Dudley who was initially going to be a welder. He was in the middle of his apprenticeship at British Steel in West Bromwich when show business snatched him away.

Most comedians will tell you that they started making people laugh when they were young. That was the case with Lenny Henry too, except that where other people were making people laugh in the playground when they were young, Henry was doing it on national television, exploding onto the national consciousness in 1975 with a triumphant performance on *New Faces*, the *X Factor* of its day.

Henry was a sixteen years old at the time and, in his over-sized, borrowed blue suit and bow-tie, did the kind of impressions any entertainer on Saturday night prime-time would do. He donned a beret and became Frank Spencer, he took it off and became Muhammad Ali. So far so ordinary, but Henry was quick to highlight his unique selling point: 'You may have seen some of these impressions before, but not in colour.' More than thirty years on Henry remains the most the most successful black entertainer Britain has ever produced.

He has been more than just a stand-up comedian. He has been a straight actor in school drama *Hope and Glory*, a sitcom

129

star in *Chef!* He has championed black comedy with his own production company, Crucial Films.

He's worked with graphic novelist Neil Gaiman. He's even found time to front a nifty funk band, Poor White Trash, as anyone who has been to his agent's Christmas parties can confirm. Nothing too serious, just Lenny on vocals and a few mates, including Hugh Laurie on keyboards.

His rise to iconic status has not been without its difficulties. Henry was part of the first generation of black British children, whose parents had left the blue-skied, sun-drenched beaches of the West Indies for life on the damp, grey streets of London, Birmingham and Coventry. In show business there were few home-grown role models. Henry himself points to the occasional appearance of actor Cy Grant on *Z Cars*. Doncaster Rovers footballer-turned-stand-up comic Charlie Williams presented the *Golden Shot* for a while, but that was about it.

Instead, Henry looked to America and picked up the albums of stand-up trailblazers Richard Pryor, Dick Gregory and Bill Cosby, who knew how to tell a story with absolute economy, making every word, every detail count. Pryor in particular left his mark: 'He made me understand how to generate material about your family and your mates,' recalled Henry in a BBC interview in 2006. But it was one thing being influenced by the great Americans, quite another following their career path. After *New Faces*, Henry's manager landed him a spot on tour. With the Black and White Minstrels.

It sounds like a bad joke now, but Henry seemed to pander to expectations. He joked that he was the only member of the cast that didn't have to black up. When he started sweating on stage he'd rub the moisture and say, 'Chocolate.' If he was heckled he'd say, 'Shut up or I'll move next door to you,' which, if it wasn't a gag from *Love Thy Neighbour*, could have been. The best things that happened during those five years was that toothy compere Don McLean (from *Crackerjack*) gave Henry some Steve Martin albums and Henry landed a part in

The Fosters, the pioneering first ITV sitcom featuring a mainly black cast.

But landing a television vehicle for his emerging stand-up comedy style was tougher. Henry could easily have slipped back into obscurity had it not been for Saturday morning children's television. When he was invited to join the team of *Tiswas* (curious fact: *Tiswas* stands for 'Today is Saturday, Wear a Smile'), there seemed to be a way out. The anarchic, loose-limbed format allowed him to be more experimental, to try out characters and to stretch himself. This meant he could mix fairly straight take-offs of such personalities as David Bellamy (on *Tiswas'* 'Compost Corner') and newsreader Trevor McDonald (who became Trevor McDoughnut), with more freewheeling creations such as Algernon Spencer Churchill Gladstone Disraeli Palmerston Pitt-The-Younger Razzamatazz, the Rastafarian with a love of bread and condensed milk sandwiches and the catchphrase, 'Ooookaaaay!' The prime-ministerial name was a nod to his family too – his parents were Winnie and Winston.

By the early eighties, however, comedy was changing. Dickie bows and frilly shirts were out, punky aggression and scruffy T-shirts were in. *Tiswas* in turn spawned a late-night adult version, *OTT*, where Henry first worked with the alternative comedy generation. He'd been to the Comedy Store, where he admired the political gags that some of the young comics were doing, and started to rethink his own approach to comedy.

Like the best black American stand-ups, alternative comedy was spawning a generation of performers who talked about themselves rather than their fictional mothers-in-law. Henry realized that he could be funny being himself and didn't always have to hide behind cartoonish characters.

The Comedy Store had another lasting effect on his life too. If this was the new comedy mafia, Henry was destined to be married to the mob. Meeting Dawn French, and then in 1984 marrying her, would cement his connection with the new

wave of acts – new, though hardly younger. It was an indication of how young Henry was when he started that he had
already been a household name for five years when he first
worked with *OTT* presenter Alexei Sayle, who was six years
older than him.

OTT was not a great success, but it did mark the arrival of a
couple of striking new characters for Henry – bad
Zimbabwean impressionist Joshua Yarlog ('Katanga!') and
pirate radio DJ Delbert Wilkins. This likeable, loud-suited
loudmouth was inspired by Lenny's older brother Seymour,
his younger brother Paul and a friend called Kevin who
would constantly say, 'You know what I mean?' The timing of
his arrival was significant too. It was in the aftermath of the
Brixton riots, with tension high between black youth and the
predominantly white police force.

The character of Wilkins proved instantly popular and
when Henry landed his own show after a stint with Tracey
Ullman and David Copperfield on *Three of a Kind*, Delbert – 'a
dandy with a bit of chat and a reputation to live up to' –
returned with a vengeance, cropping up regularly in sketches
between elderly Jamaican Deakus and bearded, blinged-up
sex god Theophilus P. Wildebeest, who brilliantly sent up the
overt sexism of libidinous soul men such as Barry White and
Alexander O'Neal.

This loveable rogue made such an impact that the second
series of *The Lenny Henry Show*, which started in October
1987, was not a sketch show at all, but a sitcom written by
Stan Hey and Andrew Nickolds, homing in on the antics of
Wilkins, who by then was running the Brixton Broadcasting
company from the room behind a south London mini-cab
office. Delbert Wilkins was a positive version of the dodgy
wise guy. This self-proclaimed 'megastar' might have been
on the legally wobbly side but he was no villain, more a
likeable rogue in the Arthur Daley mould.

Delbert was the perfect synthesis of everything Henry had
been learning since *New Faces*. He was a broad character,

certainly, but one based in truth. He had his cartoonish elements, certainly, but he was also political. In the monologue featured here, Wilkins is reflecting the experiences of any urban black man with a bit of cash in their pockets and the temerity to spend it on ostentatious motors. His routine about being stopped by the police in his flashy motor ('Are you the driver?' 'It's automatic but I have to be here') is a comic echo of the experiences of the real-life rapper who was eventually forced to sell his sports car because he was unjustly pulled over by the constabulary so often it was becoming inconvenient. This might seem like a light-hearted riff but it culminates in a climax about being tortured in a police cell. It took a comedian as powerful, subtle and charismatic as Henry to pull off this mix of hard-hitting politics and larger-than-life patter.

Henry's hit series made him a bona fide mainstream star. At the same time he was becoming a better, stronger stand-up comedian. By the late eighties, his material was unrecognizable from a decade earlier. He now had the confidence to talk about his own experiences as a first generation Jamaican. He talked about being smacked by his strict mum and also talked about racism. 'The National Front wants to give us ten pounds to go back home? Brilliant I'll take the money and go back to Dudley.'

By the late eighties he had effectively reinvented himself and had done it the hard way: in public. When Henry had been on *New Faces* all those years ago, one of the judges – Tony Hatch, who wrote the theme to *Crossroads* – had said he would not be an impressionist, he would be a storyteller, and he was right. Not that Henry wasn't averse to a good old spot of pop parody too. He famously spoofed Michael Jackson's crotch-grabbing *Bad* video, which looked almost as expensive as the original, and certainly as ludicrous.

Henry's success as a major star opened up all sort of doors. He was offered straight acting roles and even a movie deal in America with Touchstone films, which gave him a chance of emulating his heroes Pryor, Martin and Robin Williams. *True*

Identity, released in 1991, failed to set the world alight, but it did mean that Henry was able to spend more time concentrating on his stand-up career, which continued to go from strength to strength. At the start of the nineties Henry was at the peak of his powers. He never bludgeoned people with right-on references to race but it was always there: 'Stay away from ecstasy,' he warned during the height of rave culture, 'It's a drug that's so strong it makes white people think they can dance.'

Having reached this influential position, he now took it upon himself to open a few doors for other black performers. This kind of help had not been there for him and he wanted to make sure it was there for the next generation. He set up independent production company Crucial Films and through his Step Forward workshop developed the comedy show *The Real McCoy*, the first mainly black sketch show fronted by Curtis Walker and Ishmael Thomas.

Although *The Real McCoy* ran for five series, from 1991 to 1996, it never really crossed over from cult viewing to mainstream must-see. But in its own way – and this is thanks to Henry – it laid the groundwork for something that did. Two of the regular *McCoy* performers were Meera Syal and Kulvinder Ghir and they went on to star in the Anglo-Asian phenomenon *Goodness Gracious Me*.

Henry continues to champion black talent today. After his successful sojourns in acting with *Chef!* and *Hope and Glory*, he returned to the sketch format at the turn of the millennium, and has made a point of giving airtime in his series to the likes of Gina Yashere, Felix Dexter, Tameka Empson and Ninia Benjamin. He continues to be a force to be reckoned with behind the scenes.

He is at his best, however, in front of an audience. Sometimes television has not quite known what to do with Henry, which may be why he has tried so many different formats. He is clearly at his best just chatting away and he makes a brilliant talk show guest – maybe he should be a talk show host but I'm not sure if the other guests would get a word in edgeways.

As a stand-up comedian, he just gets braver and better. After his mother Winnie died in 1999, his next live tour homed in on his double life growing up in a West Indian household in the 1960s. With his family at home, he talks in patois; then, as soon as he hooks up with his mates, and on to the topic of Monty Python, he moves into a Black Country accent.

In many respects, this powerful, moving show, *So Much Things to Say*, encapsulated what Henry has managed to do over the years. His talent is fusing these two experiences, two cultures, together. He has never ignored his black experiences; instead, he has packaged them – though never in a cynical way – so that everybody can relate to them. Henry might be the finest black comedian this country has ever produced, but ultimately the colour of his skin is irrelevant. What he does is unite audiences of every creed by simply making astute comical observations the human condition. He is a master at joining up these disparate elements. Maybe he became a welder after all.

Bruce Dessau

'Delbert Wilkins'

'The Secret Policeman's Third Ball' (Amnesty gala),
London Palladium, London (1987),
Laughing Stock LAFFCD 107

What's happening?

My name is Delbert Wilkins. I come from Brixton.

Why do the police keep messing with me all the time?

It's true, guy.

All the time they keep stopping me and searching me, stopping me and searching me, stopping me and searching me. It's getting so bad, man, I'm beginning to suspect myself.

[*Laughter*]

You know, I look in the mirror and go, 'Oh, maybe I did do something.'

[*Laughter*]

'I'm sure I've seen that face on *Crime Watch*.' You know what I mean?

[*Laughter*]

I'll tell you why the police are getting so funky nowadays, right? It's because the government are trying to give the police extra powers, guy.

What for?

The police don't need any bloody extra powers. That's like putting a spear on the end of a cruise missile.

[*Laughter*]

You just don't need it. You know what I mean?

[*Laughter, applause*]

Something else this government are trying to initiate, the Neighbourhood Watch. They've got that slogan. 'Stop crime, lie about your next-door neighbour.'

[*Laughter*]

People have been getting carried away, man. They've been arresting themselves, beating themselves up, and then denying it the next day. You know what I mean? It's getting well out of order, you know?

[*Laughter*]

Something else, right, that the police don't like is when they see young black urban professionals driving a *sexy automobile*.

[*Laughter*]

Because they've got that crappy one with the red strip down the side.

[*Laughter*]

They don't like it, because I've got a brand new BMW convertible.

I converted it myself. It used to be a Ford Cortina.

[*Laughter, applause*]

The car is wicked. You know what I mean? Wide tyres, whiplash aerial, imitation leopard-skin seats. Those imitation leopards are a bugger to catch, guy. You know what I mean?

[*Laughter*]

So I'm driving down the street the other day, you know, seats reclined so far back the only way I can see is through the sunroof.

[*Laughter*]

I was navigating by the stars, guy. You know what I mean? Checking out my compact disc player. I'm not actually listening to anything, because by the time I cut all my albums up to fit in the slot they're ruined.

You know what I mean?

[*Laughter*]

So I'm driving, driving, driving, you know? That's three times. I'm driving. I'm looking in the rear view mirror, because my hair was looking wicked.

[*Laughter*]

I see this police car following me for about a mile down the street, so I pull in, because I want to talk to him.

[*Laughter*]

This young policeman swaggers over to my motor, right? He put his head through the window, which worried me, because it was still wound up at the time.

[*Laughter*]

He said, 'Are you the driver of this vehicle?' I said, 'Well, it's automatic, but I have to be here.'

[*Laughter*]

He said, 'Can you identify yourself?' I looked in the mirror. I said, 'Yep, that's me.'

[*Laughter*]

He said, 'Don't give me that bollocks, Wilkins,' because he knew me.

[*Laughter*]

He said, 'Look at this car, guy. Four bald tyres, faulty exhaust, no tax disc.' I said, 'Well, look at it this way. At least I'm wearing my seatbelt.'

[*Laughter*]

The police are bloody critical, aren't they? I mean, they never tell you when you're doing anything right, do they?

I mean, wouldn't it be nice if one day you were just driving along, suddenly a policeman flagged you down and said, 'Listen, guy, the way you took that corner was wicked.' Do you know what I mean?

[*Laughter*]

Give you a little badge or something, a little hat with 'Careful Driver' on it, some jelly or something. Instead they just hassle innocent citizens all the time.

Anyway, he arrested me.

[*Laughter*]

Took me down to the station, threw me in a cell. I said, 'Hey, are you going to charge me or what?' He said, 'What a good idea.' So they took all my clothes away and put electrodes on my nipples.

[*Laughter*]

So, a couple of minutes later, I'm standing there smouldering, you know, feeling highly charged. He kept me waiting in that cell for about seven hours, guy, while the divvy behind the desk was going through my documents, you know, with a flamethrower.

[*Laughter*]

Eventually, he said I was allowed to make one phone call.

So I rang me Uncle Desmond in Jamaica, because I hadn't spoken to him for ages.

You know what I mean?

[*Laughter*]

Thank you very much.

[*Applause*]

'Trevor Nettleford'

'The Secret Policeman's Biggest Ball' (Amnesty gala),
Cambridge Theatre, London (1989),
Laughing Stock LAFFC 20

[*Applause*]

Good evening! My name is Mr Nettleford,
Trevor Nettleford. I have an enquiring
mind.

[*Laughter*]

Cat flaps. Cat flaps. What is the sense in
cat flaps?

[*Laughter*]

Whose idea was cat flaps? How come cats
have all the flaps?

[*Laughter*]

I don't have a man flap. A little spider
doesn't have a little spider flap, so why
do cats have the monopoly on flaps?

[*Laughter*]

I hate the way they come into your house
through the cat flap, looking at you,
rubbing it in as if to say, 'Ha, ha, ha …'

[*Laughter*]

'Where's your flap then?'

[*Laughter*]

'Ah! You are flapless!'

141

[*Laughter*]

Take your cat and your flap and bugger off!

[*Laughter*]

TV shows, TV shows. Why, at the end of a TV show does the man always say, 'We'll see you at the same time next week. Don't forget to tune in'? If you tune in the same time next week, the programme will be finished.

[*Laughter*]

[*Applause*]

Where is the logic in that? What kind of sense is that?

[*Laughter*]

Take your TV show and bugger off.

[*Laughter*]

Babies. Babies. I don't trust babies; I think they're up to something.

[*Laughter*]

They're always creeping and crawling around. Stand straight like normal human beings.

[*Laughter*]

And they never talk to you, do they, babies? All this goo-goo, ga-ga. Speak bloody English!

[*Laughter*]

I don't trust babies as far as I can throw them — and that's a pretty long bloody way.

[*Laughter*]

That is why you need a babysitter. Because, if you didn't have a babysitter, the minute you leave the house they'd be on the phone ringing up for baby pizza, dancing to Fisher Price music.

[*Laughter*]

Letting all their friends in through the cat flap.

[*Laughter*]

Shag-pile carpets. What kind of name is 'shag-pile carpets'? Who thought of shag-pile carpets? What's next, bonking rugs?

[*Laughter*]

Fornicating placemats? I want to know.

James Bond. I don't trust James Bond. Every time you see him he looks different.

[*Laughter and applause*]

Everywhere he goes it blows up. He goes to China: it blows up. He goes to Russia: it blows up. He goes to Jamaica: it blows up. That's why he never goes home; if he did it would blow up.

[*Laughter*]

Every time you see James Bond, he's snogging up a woman. He goes to Jamaica: he's snogging up a woman. He goes to

LENNY HENRY

Thailand: he's snogging up a woman. He goes
to Russia: he's snogging up a woman. And
you never hear him say, 'Where's my
condoms?'

[*Laughter*]

'Shaken, not stirred — by the way, have you
got any johnnies for the weekend?'

[*Laughter*]

So there must be millions of James Bond
babies all over the world. They could be
dangerous children. You put the nappy on
them: it blow up. If you give them rusk:
they blow up. They kiss grandma: she blow
up. I don't want to be near these children!
Anyway, they don't exist. You know why?
Because every time James Bond snogs with a
woman, the next time you see her she's been
shot or strangled or drowned. This is an
extreme form of contraception …

[*Laughter and applause*]

Thank you and good night.

8. BILL HICKS

Available for children's parties

There are comedians who have scorchingly brilliant material and cannot do justice to it. There are comedians who have great technical skill but don't have the material to back it up. And then there is the late Bill Hicks who had both in abundance. The much-missed comedian has every tool in the performer's armoury and, more importantly, something to say. Make that *lots* to say. It is no surprise that, despite the fact that Hicks died of pancreatic cancer in 1994, his influence is stronger today than ever.

William Melvin Hicks was only 32 years old when he died but he was already a stand-up veteran with nearly two decades of experience under his belt. He had started gigging at the age of 13 in Houston, Texas – he was fabled to have climbed out the back window of his parents' house. At first a major influence was Woody Allen, and for a while Hicks worked in a juvenile double act with boyhood friend Dwight Slade, but he soon found his own voice, mixing topical gags with personal material. By the time he was old enough to frequent clubs and bars legally, he was a seasoned pro.

Houston, however, was simply too small to contain this subversive talent, and for a while he moved to Los Angeles, where he landed regular gigs at the legendary Comedy Store on Sunset Boulevard. Fresh-faced and fast-talking, he was soon spotted by television. In 1984, he made his first appearance on David Letterman's talk show. Much to his surprise he was also cast in a sitcom pilot entitled *Bulba*, in which he played Marine Sergeant Phil Repulski. The show didn't take off, and Hollywood's loss was comedy's gain.

Hicks returned to Houston, and in his mid-twenties had a significant following as part of a group of wild-living renegade comedians known as the Texas Outlaws. The leading light of this group was another comic who would die before his time: Sam Kinison. Kinison's delivery was blow-torch-fierce, his material angry. He'd scream his lungs out about women who had dumped him.

By comparison, Bill was the voice of reason. He quickly rose through the ranks and branched out on his own, gigging around the southern states of America. He called his never-ending road show 'The Flying Saucer Tour'. As he explained to audiences, 'I feel like a UFO because I'm appearing in obscure southern towns in front of handfuls of hillbillies, and just like the UFOs these hillbillies find me equally incomprehensible.'

The gigs frequently offered Hicks the kind of rough rides he revelled in. There was no point preaching to the converted, and the last thing he wanted was a passive, uninterested crowd. He relished a reaction. At one show he had a gun pulled on him by an irate heckler; at another he was beaten up by disgruntled audience members. It may have been on the latter occasion that members of the crowd accosted him after the show: 'Hey buddy, we're Christians and we don't like what you said about Jesus.' 'Well, forgive me, then,' he famously retorted.

His material took on an increasingly satirical tone as he lambasted everything that he despised about mainstream America. On the various official DVD and CD releases and bootlegs that have surfaced since his untimely death, you can hear Hicks grappling with a difficult crowd. On *Sane Man* (Rykodisc), filmed in 1988 at the Laff Stop in Austin – about as liberal a place as you can get in Texas, the mullet-headed front-row drinkers are resting their elbows on the stage and look like they have come for a Billy Ray Cyrus gig. Hicks has to pull out all the stops to win them over, but he rises to the challenge.

Sometimes he had to be content with a draw. In Pittsburgh in June 1990 (released as *The Flying Saucer Tour*, vol. 1, on Rykodisc), he battled with what he dubbed the worst audience he has ever had to play to. A mobile phone goes off, and he is gloriously exasperated by a 'fan' who would rather chat to a mate than pay attention. Hicks threatens to call his agent and fire him for booking him to do this show. He seemed to love it when an audience didn't understand where he was coming from and stared at him 'like a dog that's just been shown a card trick'.

When the crowds did pay attention, however, they would hear some of the sharpest, most blisteringly intelligent comedy of the last thirty years. Hicks seemed to be leagues ahead of his contemporaries in terms of ideas, ambition and sheer verve. There was an element of misanthropy certainly, but, even when Hicks was so angry about the world he was almost spitting bile, there was an underlying humanity in his voice. Like Jonathan Swift, he thought the planet was just plain mad, so jokes were the only answer. But he also thought the world was unjust. Why, for instance, was Barry Manilow still alive when John Lennon was dead?

He could talk about anything and everything, and find the comic angle where others didn't even think of looking. Routines that seem, well, routine now, had their origins in Hicks. He was one of the first humorists to pick up on the vacuity of celebrity. His diatribes against the tawdry, disposable nature of pop music are more valid than ever today – swap Britney for Debbie Gibson, and McFly for New Kids on the Block, and the jokes are box fresh again. Hicks' vivid imagination went into overdrive as he pictured his hero Jimi Hendrix chopping Debbie Gibson into little pieces with his dick. When he felt he had gone a little too close to the edge even by his standards, he always had an immaculately timed line waiting in the wings, 'I am available for children's parties by the way,' before breaking into his riff about 'Beelzebozo, the clown from hell.'

Sometimes his stories were so remarkably prescient the names don't even need to be changed to make them relevant again. After Operation Desert Storm, Hicks spoke at length about America's cunning cowboyish global policies of arming countries and then attacking them because they are armed. Fifteen years on you can replay the same gags word for word, and they sound as topical applied to the contemporary Iraq War. There just happens to be a different George Bush in the White House.

He tackled serious subjects with increasing ease. His pornography riff (featured here) is a formidable mix of sociological analysis and dick jokes. As a libertarian he argued persuasively in favour of drugs, pointing, for instance, to all the great music that had been recorded under the influence. For him, a crunching guitar solo from Keith Richards said more about the power of mind-altering substances than any television anti-narcotics advert comparing a fry-up in a pan to a brain on drugs.

He had religion nailed too. 'You ever noticed how people who believe in Creationism look really unevolved? Eyes real close together, eyebrow ridges, big furry hands and feet. "I believe God created me in one day." Yeah, looks like He rushed it.' And as for performers who advertised anything, they were creatively bankrupt in his eyes: 'You do a commercial, and you are off the artistic roll-call forever.'

Hicks' reputation built slowly in America, but in Britain his impact was almost immediate. In autumn 1990, he was part of a package of American acts that came to the Queen's Theatre, London, under the name 'Stand-up America'. Hicks was immediately acclaimed by both audiences and the press. Not for the first or last time he was compared to that other comic philosopher who excelled at saying the unsayable, Lenny Bruce.

There was another comparison too. Like Hicks' beloved Jimi Hendrix – for a time he came on stage to the strains of 'Voodoo Chile' – he was a genius who had to leave his own country to get the recognition he deserved. Hendrix had relocated to London in the late sixties. Hicks never went as far as a permanent move, but Britain would always be a special place for him. It was where his stinging critiques of corporate America were best appreciated. Back home, much of the population (the section lacking in self-awareness) never exactly embraced his humour – his 'Noam Chomsky with dick jokes'.

His timing could not have been better. The British alternative comedy scene had settled into a cosy rut. What had started out as a politically motivated movement had turned into a pension scheme for many of the original performers. Hicks had the anger and the ability to articulate that anger that British comedians lacked.

British audiences were more open to ideas, and Hicks wanted his audience to think about what he was saying rather than merely laugh. 'Can I recommend some jugglers you might like?' he once said to an interviewer who kept questioning him about why his material had to be so challenging, so uncompromising. 'I don't want butts in the seats, I want minds in the room.'

I first saw Bill Hicks at the Edinburgh Fringe Festival in 1991. He was playing a large venue called The Spiegeltent, a temporary circus top with mirrors around the sides. Needless to say, it was a mesmerizing performance that lived up to every expectation. Hicks delivered his well-honed solid-gold material with absolute confidence. In front of an appreciative audience, he was in control from start to finish. Where other comedians might race through their acts, he was in such command he could vary the pace however he liked. He would pause, think, turn his back on the crowd, wait for a laugh he knew would come eventually, or simply stop talking and light one of his umpteen cigarettes.

There was an intensity on stage that night that was palpable. But then everything Hicks did, he did with intensity. When he got into drugs, he seriously got into drugs. When he cleaned up, he became a passionate advocate of

149

smoking. On stage he'd take out a cigarette, gaze at then non-smokers with undisguised contempt, and brag about his nicotine habit: 'You know you smoke too much when other smokers tell you to put it out,' he fumed at his audience. He was such a heavy smoker he was on two lighters a day. And with a twinkle in his eye, he broke some bad news to those that resisted the lure of the death stick: 'Non-smokers die every day.' Oh, and he was also very good at bog-standard observational gags: 'What did moths bump into before light bulbs were invented?'

In 1992 I interviewed Hicks. His outlook seemed a little bleak, but he was all the more hilarious for it. He had just recorded his album *Arizona Bay*, in which he talked about his hope that Los Angeles would soon sink into the Pacific, where it belonged. On that positive note, I asked him if he was in a long-term relationship: 'I can't even keep my house-plants alive,' he joked. Comedy was an all-consuming process for Hicks.

By 1993 his career had really begun to take off. He was regularly touring Britain, and talking about making a television series for Channel 4, entitled *Counts of the Netherworld*, in which he and another comedian sat in a mocked-up Victorian salon discussing the issues or the day and putting the world to rights. Even America was finally catching on to him, and he had been named 'Hot Stand-Up Comic' by *Rolling Stone* magazine.

But Hicks' health was failing. It was not the cigarettes that had done him in, as one might have expected. In a cruel twist, he was diagnosed with pancreatic cancer. This seemed to galvanize him: in his final year he worked harder than ever, gigging as much as he could, while reading and writing whenever he had a moment to spare.

On 1 October 1993, he was booked to appear on The Letterman Show for the twelfth time. He filmed his routine which included his searing polished piece about anti-abortionists (that if they are so pro-life they should lock arms and surround cemeteries), and was told everything was fine. Then, when the programme went out, he had been cut. The truth has never been confirmed, but it has been alleged that because pro-lifers advertised during the programme the network decided to cut his contentious material out (curious fact: one of Hicks' staunchest supporters was *New Yorker* critic John Lahr, the son of Bert Lahr, who played the Cowardly Lion in *The Wizard of Oz*).

Hicks was incandescent. He thought he had a good relationship with Letterman, and felt betrayed. He already had contempt for corporate America; now he regarded Letterman as part of the problem too, rather than a little chink of light in a dark business, where even the tea-boys had sold their souls to Satan.

Sadly, Hicks wasn't able to pursue the matter for much longer. He continued to perform live as often as his health allowed, with his performances as committed as ever. When he wasn't able to continue touring, he returned to his home in Little Rock, Arkansas, where he died on 26 February 1994.

Twelve years later, there are a couple of tantalizing questions. What would Hicks be doing if he were alive today? Well, presumably not advertising Coke, Pepsi or even cigarettes, although I'm sure the corporate machine would have tried to buy him. Maybe he would have got his own chat show on a cable network. One which gave him absolutely editorial freedom, maybe scheduled it against Letterman. I can't somehow see him returning to the island of *Bulba*.

Then there is the question of what kind of material he would be doing. It would be great to hear Hicks on 9/11, iPods, or Janet Jackson's nipple popping out. Though, of course, we can always go back to his CDs and DVDs to hear what he said about George Bush.

Then again, at times it feels as if Hicks is still with us. Glance at the cinema listings and Michael Moore is banging his anti-corporate drum. In the rock world, Radiohead have name checked him. Henry Rollins captures some of the intensity in his spoken-word shows. Hicks is there in Daniel Kitson's refusal to compromise and exemplary stagecraft. He is there in the political agenda of Robert Newman. He is there is the controlled anger of Stewart Lee. And there are many others who have been influenced by him.

Hicks had the humble aim of wanting to make the world a better place. In changing the face of modern comedy, I think he succeeded.

Bruce Dessau

'What is Pornography?'

The Laff Stop, Austin (1991),
Laughing Stock LAFFCD 107
Excerpted from BILL HICKS Relentless (RCD 10351)

That's the problem with this country, one of many, but this … this whole issue of sexuality and pornography, which I don't understand what pornography is, I really don't. To me, pornography is, you know, spending all your money and not educating the people of America, but spending it instead on weapons. That's pornographic to me. That's totally filthy [*Applause*] and etcetera, etcetera, down the line. You all in your fucking hearts know the goddamn arguments. Okay, okay.

But no one knows what pornography is.

Supreme Court says pornography is any act that has no artistic merit and causes sexual thoughts. That's their definition essentially. No artistic merit. Causes sexual thought. Hmm. Sounds like every commercial on television, doesn't it?

[*Laughter, applause*]

You know, when I see those two twins on that Doublemint commercial, I'm not thinking of gum.

[*Laughter*]

I *am* thinking of chewing. Maybe that's the connection they're trying to make.

[*Laughter*]

You've all seen that Busch Beer commercial.
The girl in the short hot-pants opens the
beer bottle on her belt buckle, leaves it
there and it foams over her hand and over
the bottle and the voiceover goes, get
yourself a Busch.

[*Laughter*]

Hmm. You know what that looks like? Nah, no
way.

[*Laughter*]

I'll tell you the commercial they'd like to
do if they could, and I guarantee you, if
they could, they'd do this right here.
Here's the woman's face, beautiful. Camera
pulls back. Naked breasts. Camera pulls
back. She's totally naked, legs apart, two
fingers right here, and it just says,
'Drink Coke.

[*Laughter*]

Now, I don't know the connection here, but
goddamn if Coke isn't on my shopping list
that week. Dr Pepper … [*Laughter*] Snickers
satisfying … [*Laughter*] Damned if I'm not
buying these products. My teeth are rotting
out of my head. I'm glued to the television.
I'm as big as a fucking couch. [*Laughter*]

More Snickers.

More Coke.

That's what I find ironic too, is that
people who are against these things that

cause sexual thoughts are generally fundamentalist Christians who also believe you should be *fruitful* and *multiply*. Boy, they walk a tightrope every day, don't they? How do we be fruitful and multiply and not think about it?

We could sing hymns during it. One stroke at a time, sweet Jesus.

[*Laughter*]

One stroke at a time, sweet Lord … I did that joke in Alabama, in Phyffe, and these three rednecks met me after the show. 'Hey, buddy, come here. [*Laughter*] Mr Funny Man, come here. Hey, buddy, we're Christians. We don't like what you said …'

I said, 'Then forgive me.'

[*Applause*]

Later, when I was hanging from the tree …

[*Laughter* and *applause*]

from BILL HICKS 'Salvation'

Oxford, November 11, 1992 (RCD 10833)

I was here during the riots. That was
weird. That was the last time I was here.
This time there's an election. Last time, a
riot. I came over the day the riots
happened, too. That was what was so weird
about it. I left LA:

'Bye Bill, enjoy England.'

'I will, y'all have fun while I'm gone.'

'We will, Bill. Bye. Bye. Bye. See you.
Bye-bye.'

Land at Heathrow Airport eleven hours
later, pass a newspaper stand: 'LA Burns to
Ground.' Shit, did I leave a cigarette lit?
How much are these? See if my picture's in
here. Right, and I'm over here, trying to
get news of the riots, right? You got four
channels, all four are playing *snooker* for
no fucking apparent reason. What is this?
Different angles of the table? 'For
north/south coverage of snooker, turn to
BBC2. For east/west coverage of snooker,
turn to BBC1. For the overhead view, turn
to BBC3. For a look under Jimmy White's
left arm, turn to Channel 4.' You're going,
'Duh, how much longer are you gonna
continue that impression, Bill? Any more in
the act?' [*Laughs*]

Who is this guy Jimmy White? Last time I was here: riots. I turn on the TV; there was snooker: Jimmy White. Nine months earlier, the last thing I saw when I left the hotel room, turned the TV off before I did, what's that? Jimmy fucking White. Does this guy have a bad home life or something? Let's get him *home*. Let's iron that vest. I mean, I like snooker, don't get me wrong, you know. I think it's a little slow, you know. Perhaps could use ah some livening up. You know what snooker could use? Riot. That'd be cool, cues … But I've figured out why it's so long, man. It's 'cos this little fucking old guy — not the two players — this little old guy keeps taking the balls out of the pockets and putting them back on. 'Hey, you asshole. He got it in. Let's go! The game's almost over. He has to come over again … It's gonna take all fucking night.'

So I'm trying to get news of the riots. Nothing but snooker on, right, and ah all my friends here trying to sympathize with me. 'Oh, Bill, crime is horrible. If it's any consolation, Bill, crime is horrible here too.' 'Shut up. This is Hobbiton and I'm Bilbo Hicks, OK? You live in a fairyland. Fucking crime. I was reading the papers here. You have crimes like: "Yesterday some hooligans knocked over a dustbin in Shaftesbury." The hooligans are loose. The hooligans are loose. What if they become ruffians? I would hate to be a dustbin in Shaftesbury tonight. [*Singing*] No one knows what it's like to be a dustbin

… in Shaftesbury … with hooligans.' It's such a stupid word, you know? Hooligan. Very unthreatening word. I don't even know what a hooligan is. I think I could take twenty or thirty of 'em. I picture these real pale guys in penny loafers and no socks. 'We're the hooligans.' *Pop!* Ow, you fucker. Come here. 'No, have to catch us. You corner me, I might become a scallywag. I'm a ne'er do well.' There was something in the paper yesterday: 'Some hooligans caused a rumpus.' Not quite the same as Crip and Blood … that's a little more cutting. Little more telling. Blood. Hooligan. Bloods versus the hooligans.

Pop!

'Hey man, what you doin' motherfucker. Come 'ere.'

'Got to catch us!'

'Yeah, I'm trying that now. [*Gunshots*] There … catch your skinny pale ass. How's that?'

'Ow, he got me in the rumpus. The Blood hit me in the rumpus.'

You know, Crip, Blood, rumpus. No, I don't know. You do not have crime like we have, and you should be very grateful. Our crime is like: 'Yesterday a student beheaded his teacher. Named "Best in the Class".' Holding up the head …

I love talking about the Warren Committee. I love talking about the Kennedy assassination. I really love it, man. I was just down in Dallas, Texas … and ah you can actually go … to the School Book Depository on the sixth floor. It's a museum … called the Assassination Museum. And they have the window set up to look exactly like it did on that day. And it's really accurate, 'cos … Oswald's not in it. Incredible, painstaking detail. I don't know who did the research, but I applaud them. But it's true. It's called the Sniper's Nest, and you know, the boxes are set up, it's glassed in, you can't actually get to the window. And the reason they did that, of course, is they didn't want thousands of tourists every year, you know, coming through to the window, going, 'No way.' Yeah, that would have started this *truth* inertia happening. Who knows when it would've stopped. But there's no way. I mean, you can get to the window next to it, and you look down, you go, 'I can't see the fucking *road* from here, man.' There's a tree right here. There's no way, unless Oswald was hanging by his toes … upside down from the window ledge. *Surely* someone woulda *seen* that? Either that or some pigeons grabbed on to him and flew him over the motorcade. You know, there was rumours of anti-Castro pigeons seen drinking in bars … the week before the assassination. Someone overheard them saying, 'Coup, coup. Coup …'

People say, 'It's so weird.' You wouldn't believe the attitude in America. 'Bill, quit talking about Kennedy, man. Let it go. K? It was a long time ago. Would you just forget

it?' I'm like, 'All right. Then don't bring
up Jesus to me … Well, long as we're talking
shelf life here.' 'Bill, you know Jesus died
for you.' Yeah, yeah, it was a long time
ago. Let it go. Forget about it. How about
this: let's get Pilate to release the
fucking files. Quit washing your hands and
release the piles, Filate. Piles, Filate?
Piles, Filate. Don't worry, don't worry.
Everything's alright.

I want you to know this is the longest I've
ever gone without a cigarette in my fucking
life, and ah, no. Actually I quit smoking,
so ah … [*Audience complain*] Hey, hey! This
ain't Dylan goes electric. Chill out, all
right? 'Judas! Traitor!' People ask the
weird— 'Why d'you quit smoking?' Is that a
weird question only to me? 'Why d'you take
your mouth off the exhaust pipe, man? You
were almost there. Traitor! Judas!' I'm far
from reformed, all right? I mean, I mean,
they look good to me, I tell ya. It's hard.
It's really hard. After you eat at a
restaurant, people light up around ya. Man,
they look good. Everyone one of 'em looks
like it was made by God, rolled by Jesus,
and moistened shut with Claudia Schiffer's
pussy right now. [*Sucking sounds*] 'Golly,
that looks tasty.' It's very hard. I don't
know how to quit. My friends recommended
this thing called a patch. I don't know if
you get this here? The patch. It's like a
nicotine Band-Aid you wear, and I don't see
how it works, you know, unless you wear it
over your mouth. [*Makes muffled noise*]

'What's he saying?'

'I think he wants a cigarette.'

[*Makes muffled noise*]

'Put it up your nose?'

'I don't think the patch is helping him any.'

'Least he's not gaining weight.'

I was walking through Central Park and I saw an old man smoking. Nothing makes a smoker happier than to see an *old* person smoking. This guy was ancient, bent over a walker, puffing away, I'm just, 'Dude! You're my hero! Guy your age smoking, man. It's great.' He goes, 'What? I'm twenty-eight …'

I was worried for a while, man, the polls, you know? I was over here when you went through the Labour/Tory poll situation. That was … I was so afraid that was gonna happen back home, man. Labour ahead, Labour ahead, Labour ahead, Labour ahead, cool, it looks like it's Labour ahead! FUCK YOU! WRONG! WRONG! DEATH TO YOUR DREAMS AND HOPES! THE RAMPAGING ELEPHANT HAS FRIENDS! [*Trumpets like an elephant*] See, I wonder how real this whole thing is, man. You know, did people actually get in there, vote with their fucking wallets again? Or did they *vote* for Labour, and then that fucking old guy from the snooker game go over and take their votes? 'There will be no changes. Your hopes will remain just that.' The polls — I'm sick of the polls. Cut 'em out. They're

not funny. Quit it. You know, and they're,
they're so misleading. I saw one on CNN one
time: How many people disapprove of George
Bush's handling of the country? Seventy per
cent. Of these same people, how many will
vote for him again in November? Seventy per
cent. What the fuck? Where did they take
that at? Some S&M parlour? 'Ow! More. Ow,
keep going. Ow, don't stop.' I've never been
in an S&M parlour. You get the fucking
point. It's my white-boy, suburb fucking
impression of S&M. Requires bending over, I
don't know. [*Laughs*] I'm just so … right on
the money. But these polls, you know, they
get the answers they want by how they ask
the questions, you know what I mean? Like
during the Persian Gulf War, we would hear
questions like:

  'Do you think George Bush, a good
  Christian white man … should send troops
  to Iraq to stem the brown, Islamic tide
  from coming over here and fucking your
  daughter?'

  'I'd like to say I'm *for* this war.'

  'Ninety-eight per cent of all Americans
  support the war.'

  'This just in!'

Guess who was in that two fucking per cent?

Actually, I was for the war, I was just
against the troops, and ah … I didn't like
those young people. I was all for the
carnage, don't get me wrong, I *am* an
American. Americans love carnage, we love

death, folks, it's a — what do they say? An
ecstasy and violent fucking dream America
is. NRA — National Rifle Association — love
the LA riots. They *love* the LA riots. You
shoulda seen them on TV. Oh, man, during
the riots they're on TV: 'Ah! A-ha ha!
Yeah! Uh-huh! Ha ha!' That's about as
literate as they can be, but … I think what
the fine, Neanderthal, redneck fella was
trying to get across in his own inimitable
grunting way … I actually heard one of 'em
say, 'See, yeah! See, now how do you feel?
The mob comin' and you — no gun. Ah? Ha ha!
Here come the mob: you … no gun. How does
that feel?' See, before I bought a gun, I'd
try to figure out what it is about me that
keeps track of the fucking mobs, man.
That's the way I'd work the problem. After
all, I might run out of ammo one day. Have
to talk to these fellas …

Our last export was the Madonna Sex Book.
Did you see that? Did you have the same
effect it had on me as you? Almost a jaw-
breaking fucking yawn? [*yawns sleepily*]
That's it? That's the whole book? OK, Bye-
bye. Bye-bye. It's pretty good? Yeah, it's
OK. Twenty-five pounds for that thing? Man,
for twenty-five pounds you can actually
have sex. *Twice* if you're in Cowley. I
don't know why I keep mentioning that. I
had to do a radio show over there, and I
just started … I just … found Alabama of the
fucking Britain, sort of, you know. Wow!
'This is where Oscar Wilde went to school.'
Cowley? 'No, across the river.' Oh, OK.

9. SEAN HUGHES

Laugh at first sight

I've seen a lot of comedy shows over the years. But only a few have knocked me sideways or left me gasping for breath with delight. Some of these were gigs too embarrassing for a comedy fan with any self-respect to admit to; others have gone down in comedy history as landmark moments. Here is a quick rundown:

1) Rik Mayall and Ade Edmondson, Comedy Store, London, 1979. The comedy equivalent of the Sex Pistols at the 100 Club. A handful of fans, a lot of drunks and one exasperated punch line that still reverberates down the years: 'A fucking gooseberry in a lift!'

2) Ben Elton, Colston Halls, Bristol, 1988. Hard to believe now, but Elton really was the voice of disillusioned Britain for a couple of months. Sustained comedy ranting at its best. 'Double seat, double seat, gotta get a double seat.'

3) Reeves and Mortimer, Goldsmith's Tavern, New Cross, London, 1988. The comedy world is about to turn upside down. Vic Reeves is Heinz Mindpeeler, mentalist extraordinaire with his 'all-seeing egg'.

4) Bill Hicks, Spiegeltent, Edinburgh, 1991. There's a whole chapter on him in this book …

5) Daniel Kitson, a pub in Blackfriars, London, 2000. Six people in the audience; Jimmy Carr at the bottom of the bill. The future Perrier Award winner – without a doubt

164

the most naturally gifted comedian of his generation – decides to have a lock-in and perform a private two-hour gig, grinding a few stragglers that have joined us into submission.

6) Billy Connolly. As good as ever at the infamous 'Ken Bigley' gig at the Carling Apollo, Hammersmith, London, 2004. A non-stop whirlwind of ideas, very few misses among the hits, no toilet breaks in a two-hour-plus show.

7) Stewart Lee, Edinburgh, 2004. A master class in comic restraint.

And then there is:

8) Sean Hughes, Hen & Chickens Theatre, Highbury Corner, London, July 1990 …

The flip-up chairs are a bit rickety and the venue is half full: this is an Edinburgh Festival preview. Now, previews can be shambolic affairs at the best of times. I've seen performers read their lines off scraps of paper, or not even have lines to read. *A One Night Stand with Sean Hughes*, however, was a fully-realized piece of heartfelt stand-up comedy theatre, in which he sat in his onstage bedsit, pottered around, worried, made phone calls and talked about his beloved Morrissey. Whereas other comedians simply told jokes, Hughes perfectly fused a neurotic indie pop sensibility with a narrative – while still remembering to include plenty of one-liners. It was laugh at first sight. A month later the 24-year-old vegetarian Irishman with the crooked teeth became the youngest performer to win the Perrier Award.

Since his Edinburgh victory, Hughes' career has peeled off in all sorts of different directions. There was the inspired deconstructed Channel 4 sitcom, *Sean's Show*, in which he used the bedsit device of his Edinburgh show but took things to extreme conclusions. He mucked about with the plot, referenced Kurosawa's *Rashomon* and Julian Cope, and took great delight in addressing the audience. Anything could happen in *Sean's Show*, and most things did. He had a pet spider called Elvis, and there was even an appearance from God's lesser known brother Shaw. It was fantastic. And even better if you'd never seen *It's Gary Shandling's Show*, which played with the sitcom format in a similar way.

Then there is the writing: *Sean's Book* (Pavilion), *The Grey Area* (Pavilion), *It's What He Would Have Wanted* (Simon & Schuster) and *The Detainees* (Simon & Schuster). If sitcom allowed him to be juvenile, Hughes was far more serious in print: autobiographical flashes hinted that there was a dark side to his working-class Catholic Dublin suburb upbringing. Even in his stand-up there were nods in this direction, particularly when he mimed his dad thrashing him across the livingroom, the slaps dished out in rhythm with the words like a beatbox.

There were also the appearances as team captain on *Never Mind the Buzzcocks* for six, (yes, six) years, and acting in amiable ITV crime drama *The Last Detective,* and on stage in the West End with Sienna Miller in *As You Like It.* He also starred in a film version of Spike Milligan's *Puckoon,* which was not the greatest literary adaptation in recent years, but then Milligan is not the easiest person to adapt. Some of these projects have surely been pick-up-the-cheque jobs; others have been interesting departures. Some have reflected Hughes' enduring enthusiasm for music – for a long-time he and Mark Lamarr seemed to spending more time at indie gigs than comedy nights.

But perhaps he chooses to be wide-ranging, because he dislikes being pigeonholed. As he says in *The Grey Area,* 'We end up spending our lives in pigeon-holes where only a few dimensions of our personality are allowed to flourish.'

Hughes has done the usual stints at the Melbourne Comedy Festival and Canada's Just for Laughs. He was acclaimed at both, even though his skewed, sweet-and-sour humour didn't always translate when he was on the promotional trail, speaking to people who had never heard of him in the hope that it might shift a few tickets. In an interview with an Australian DJ, Hughes told his gag about how he was very anti-drugs because he'd once OD'd on amphetamines '… and was rushed to hospital and made to work the nightshift'. The DJ thought he was being serious.

But he seemed to fall out of love with stand-up in the late nineties. If you caught Hughes live in recent years, it would be more likely to be at a book reading. It is hard to know why he shied away. Like one of his favourite obscure bands who suddenly found themselves rocketing from cult to *Top of the Pops*, he undoubtedly felt uncomfortable about the teenage adulation, but if he had stuck with stand-up hopefully his audience would have matured with him, as they have done with Stewart Lee.

As Hughes became more successful – and richer – his material reflected his new status, but retained that vein of innocence that made him so appealing. When he talked about buying his first house in north London, he explained how he liked to run regularly into every corner of each room, to get value for money on his mortgage.

It is a shame Hughes doesn't do much stand-up any more, because he is a terrific wordsmith, with a gimlet eye for detail and crafted construction that few can match. His routines featured here, dating from 1996, capture him on blinding form trying to get to grips with techno and clubbing as a thirty-something: 'People who go to night-clubs are people who can't get sex and want to simulate it for six hours.' He is bemused by everything, from the hats, to the bouncers, to the baggy trousers. Particularly the baggy trousers.

Winning the Perrier did not represent overnight success. I had seen Hughes on the bill at umpteen London clubs in the previous couple of years. He had been doing much the same material without knitting it together quite so skilfully. Yet even in his early days his superficially simple jokes concealed a savage undertow. They would pick up an easy laugh, but there was always something more going on under the surface.

According to *Sean's Book,* one of the jokes in his first-ever set was, 'It's always a bit sad going home to visit my parents, there was always tears at the doorstep but this time they let me in.' He explains that this was one of his jokes that he got bored with because it wasn't true, but it seems to fit into a pattern of slightly sinister gags about his childhood that weave in and out of his work. Rumours suggest that he has a dysfunctional side, but then what generously gifted latter-day jester does not?

Hughes was the first Irishman to win the Perrier Award, but around that time he was not alone. Irish comedians seemed to flock to London's comedy clubs and quickly built up reputations as terrific natural performers, who could effortlessly command the stage in the roughest of venues. I remember tombstone-faced Michael Redmond having an audience in stitches without even saying anything. He was so instinctively funny even his silences were hilarious. Kevin McAleer was another master of the art of the meaningful pause.

By the late nineties the trickle had become a flood. In 1996, Dylan Moran won the Perrier when he was even younger than Hughes. In 1998, the winner was Tommy Tiernan, who came from Navan, the same town as Moran (curious fact: Pierce Brosnan also hails from Navan and was very funny in the 2005 movie *Matador* – perhaps there is something in the water ...) In the same period nominees included Graham Norton, Jason Byrne and Ed (no relation) Byrne. Ardal O'Hanlon might have won it, but he was scooped up by television and made famous and thus ineligible by *Father Ted.* Patrick Kielty might have done well in Edinburgh, but after a brief sojourn doing grotty clubs he sold his soul to reality TV, and there are no refunds on that Faustian pact.

Someone once observed that Ireland is good at producing just two things: Eurovision Song Contest winners and boy bands. In fact, it has also done quite well at Nobel Prize winners – and now stand-up comedians too can be added to the list. But why? Well, there are no concrete answers, but certainly plenty of theories.

Is it the long-standing oral tradition of yarn-spinning that has made the Irish such good comic storytellers? According to myth, you can't walk into a pub in Dublin without being told three comical tales before you even get to the bar. There is probably a grain of truth in this. After all, there wasn't much in the way of television in Ireland until Sky elbowed its way in, so in recent years people had to find other ways of entertaining each other. If this were the whole story, of course, there ought now to be a decline in the seemingly inexorable rise of Irish stand-ups. But I can't say I've noticed younger Irish comedians suddenly becoming any less good.

Dylan Moran has noted that the Irish do seem to make their own entertainment in an informal way, perfect for the all-important London comedy circuit. There is no tradition of vaudeville in Ireland, for instance. Instead, it is a case of people getting up on tiny makeshift stages and shooting the breeze. Not much different to many of the venues at the Edinburgh Festival then, where Irish performers certainly seem perfectly at home. It was not a coincidence, of course, that in Annie Griffin's 2005 film *Festival*, the winner of the fictional version of the Perrier was a tousled-haired, egocentric, ambitious Irishman – probably what you'd get if you put the DNA of Hughes, Tiernan and Moran in a test tube, shook it for twenty-four hours, and then made an uber-Irish comic out of the results.

The Irish certainly have a penchant for the surreally comic when it comes to literature. Samuel Beckett's *Waiting for Godot* is essentially about two clowns passing the time of day in an existential reverie. If you have the discipline to get through James Joyce's *Ulysses*, I think you'll find it is a free-wheeling comic novel. And Flann O'Brien, with his people and bicycles blurring into one big atomic bundle, had a comic mind equal in fertility to that of any stand-up. Maybe these days aspiring novelists have realized that a comedy profile is a grand way of landing a literary agent and a lucrative book deal. Ardal O'Hanlon has also followed Hughes into print, and Dylan Moran must surely publish a book at some point.

There's another theory. Irish Catholics tend to come from big families. Therefore you have to develop a way with words and cultivate a certain presence to make yourself heard: two skills which would certainly stand you in good stead at the Comedy Store at the midnight show on a Friday night, when the front row comprises a stag party from Wandsworth. (In this case, the gifted Owen O'Neill, who co-wrote and co-starred in the play *Patrick's Day* with Hughes, ought to be the biggest star on the planet, as he is one of sixteen siblings.)

How relevant all of this is to Sean Hughes, however, is open to debate. In fact, there is a twist to his tale. Apparently, in 1965, he was born plain 'John Hughes' – in London. He only moved back to Ireland when he was five, and for the first couple of years had to put up with being regularly thumped for sounding like a cockney. No wonder he developed an Irish accent and changed his name to 'Sean'. But whether he's actually part of the Green Wave is the real Irish Question here.

Given his name-change and a cameo in *The Commitments* as the boss of a label with the delightful moniker Eejit Records ('A small but pivotal role,' he once told me), however, let us include him in the thesis. In which case he is the ultimate exemplar of another thing that makes a great comic. He sees things as an outsider. In the same way that, according to Arnold Brown, Jews make great comics because they never quit fit in and have a slightly dislocated perspective. Hughes too sees things differently.

And so this ardent Crystal Palace-loving refusenik remains determined to go his own way. Not English, but not quite part of the Irish invasion either. Doing his own thing. In summer 2006 I heard he was doing some try-out gigs. Just testing the waters in a small London venue with a view to some possible stand-up shows in the future. Prior commitments meant I didn't manage to go. Shame really. He was back at the Hen & Chickens. Where it all began for Sean and me.

Bruce Dessau

from 'Alibis for Life'

Melbourne International Comedy Festival,
Melbourne Town Hall (1998),
Laughing Stock LAFFCD 83

No, 'cos like I want, I want responsibility
in my life. I want to settle down with X. I
want to have kids. I want the big fucking
bunch of keys. You know what I'm talking
about? The keys of responsibility. You see
the people with the jingle jangle of
responsibility that go, 'Look at all these
keys, I don't know what half these keys
do.' [Laughter]. 'I've never seen this key
before but someone gave it to me 'cos they
trust me 'cos I'm responsible. I've got the
look of responsibility'. [Laughter].

You see, with Matt and Diane like, I hope
the relationship doesn't fall apart 'cos
they've got the kid and the kid gives them
responsibility. Even though they always say
it hasn't, every time I call around to
their house Matt goes, 'Sean, nothing's
changed between me and you. We can still
have those wild and crazy times we've
always had.' And I'm thinking, yeah, then
how come I'm smoking outside in the fucking
garden?' [Laughter].

Also, I feel sorry for my parents 'cos they
want grandchildren 'cos all their friends
have got grandchildren and they think
they're freaks and I go, 'Mom, you're not a

freak, I'm the freak, just tell them that, would you? [*Laughter*]

But they're desperate for grandchildren and dad keeps on dropping little subtle hints like … 'Fuck *her*.' [*Laughter*]. Last time I saw him he handed me a beaker and said, 'Look, just do it into that. We'll take care of everything else'.

But I don't know if they even want grandchildren. They just want to be able to take something out of their wallet and show their friends and go, 'Look, we're normal too.' So, for Christmas I sent them over four morning-after pills and they had two little faces on them and everything. Like that would have been Timmy, that would have been Mary-Anne. 'You pick a name, dad, they're your grandchildren'. Have a blast. Why not? Choose life … [*Laughter*]

This is where I thank you for coming tonight. I really do respect you, you know, and love you for paying money in to see me and I hope it goes beyond that. I hope it isn't just a, you know, a money give me type vibe for humour. I hope we're, you know, we're sharing a moment tonight which I'll remember for the rest of my life and hopefully you will as well. [*Sobs*] So, why am I so cynical? I didn't mean that. I had to spoil it there by saying something stupid like, hoppita, holla, dingo, dingo time …

No, I do and, and specially tonight. Anyone over the age of 30 who's turned up, much

respect because once you hit 30 the idea of
leaving your house is pretty fucking weird,
isn't it? [*Laughter*] 'Shall we go out
tonight? Whatever for? We've got a
television, video, CDs, booze, food, each
other, what the fuck are you talking
about'? [*Laughter*]

'Anyway, I've triple-locked that door.
There's no way I'm undoing that, [*Laughter*]
and the dingo might get us.' Obviously, if
you're single, you have to leave the house
on occasion because they always say the
perfect person could be just around the
corner, so I just walk around the block
once a day … [*Laughter*]

But it's weird as well once you're, once
you're over 30 and you're still single,
because no matter what age you are, on a
first date you have to be 17. You know, you
can be a 65-year-old mum, on the first date
you have to be 17 — bubbly and enthusiastic
and care about them and ask questions about
their friends …

And to be fair, I can't afford that much
cocaine. [*Laughter*].

We're going out on a date. Hang on one sec.
[*Sniffs, then speaking at top speed*] So,
these are your friends then. 'How are you
doing? Pleased to meet you. So you work in
a bank, do you?' Tell me all about that
then, would you? [*Laughter*] 'So, with the
uniform, do you have to take that home and
clean it yourself or do they clean it to
make sure it's pristine?' Come back. I want

to talk to you … 'You know that when you
have that pen on a bit of a string in the
bank? We're supposed to trust you with all
our money but you don't trust us with a
pen? What the fuck's going on there, my
friend?' [*Laughter*]. Eh? Come back. I've
more to say to you, you know. 'How come
like you take your lunch between 12:00 and
2:00 when that's the fucking busiest time
of day when everybody's going to the bank?
What the fuck's going on there?' [*Laughter,
sniffs again*]

Oh, it's hard work, relationships. Like
even like the … There's that killing time
as well, the first time where you go away
for the weekend. You're going, 'Shall we go
away for the weekend? My fucking nostril's
numb here.' [*Laughter*] And she says, 'Sure
… We've been seeing each other now for six
months and you're always really randy. Any
chance you might ejaculate at some point?'
[*Laughter, sniffs*]. Wouldn't think so, no …
Is that important? If I take my penis out,
the dingo might get it.' I do run with a
joke, don't I folks … [*Laughter*]

Now, if you're in a couple I suggest … It
keeps on coming back to me, I'm trying hard
to concentrate, I suggest you don't need to
do cocaine if you're in a relationship. In
fact, I'd say if you do take it you soon
realize, you know, there's no alternative
to your lifestyle, and that makes life even
harder, okay? [*Laughter*] My little bit of
advice …

But there's other drugs. If you're in a relationship a couple tranquillizers is quite a good one. [*Laughter*]. Feel a row coming on, pop a pill. Ba ba ba ba.

'Have you ever taken E, my friend? [*Asks man in audience*] No? No. You weren't sure there, were you? [*Laughter*] 'Have you taken it, though? You have, haven't you? You have.' You see, I should be a cop, shouldn't I? [*Laughter*]. See how fucking easy it is. So in all of these cop shows they play good cop, bad cop … You just have to ask the question *again*, [*Laughter*] and like imply that you already know the answer. 'Ah, you have done, haven't you?' 'Yeah, I have.' [*Laughter*]

I think the other thing the cops should do is *give* these people they are questioning cocaine 'cos if you give them cocaine they'll fucking tell you anything anyway. [*Laughter*]

'Did you kill the person?' 'No.' 'Have a line of coke.' [*Sniffs*] 'Yeah, that's fucking great, I got the knife, right. It was fucking great.' [*Laughter*]. 'Fucking great like … Can I get some more?' 'No. Not until you get to prison. Then you can have as much as you want.'

But, see, I've never taken ecstasy myself because I'm … We didn't have any when I was 19 and it's a young person's drug. When I was 19 we just had paracetamol, you know, and I was fucking crazy for that stuff, you know. [*Laughter*]

'Going clubbing tonight?' 'Yes, I am.' 'Do you want a P?' 'Yes, I bloody do.' [*Laughter*]. 'The music's quite loud, can I have another one? Thank you very much.' And also we didn't have … We couldn't have ecstasy when I was 19 because we didn't have the music. You know, you need all that *beep beep* music. You can't take ecstasy and then go … 'Everybody was kung fu fighting …' [*Audience applause*] 'Everybody was kung fu …' That's not going to get you loved up, is it?

Heroin, now that's such a clichéd drug. 'You're probably on that all the time, yeah?' [*Asks man in audience again*] You know, its such a clichéd drug. I once watched two friends shooting up heroin … I was quite shocked, 'cos they didn't have Scottish accents for a start, you know. [*Laughter*]

It kind of threw me a little bit. But now they're there and they took this heroin and it went up their veins and their eyes glazed over in unison and they turned to me and went, 'Sean, this is like the best orgasm ever,' and I'm thinking … 'Not great then.' [*Laughter*] All I'm thinking is the amount of money I've saved over the years by masturbating, you know. Put that in a jar, have a little holiday for myself maybe. [*Laughter*]

What's your name, by the way? Dave. And you're married and stuff, yeah? You see, this is the thing that I really appreciate.

Because what you have and I could never have … is extra-marital affairs. [*Laughter*]

'Cos dating is all very well, isn't it? Let's do this, let's do that, da da da da da da da, but extra-marital affairs is, oh my God, if I fuck this person I fuck all of this up. Yeah, I'll go for it. [*Laughter*] And also like … thanks again for coming to the show, because usually couples with kids and stuff they only ever leave the house for emergencies, you know, shopping and shelving …

'Oh my God, our lives are so dull, we've amassed so much stuff, we're going to need some more shelves. What are we going to do?' [*Laughter*] 'Right. You go to Ikea, I'll cover you. Go, go, go, go, go.' Because there's all those single people out there are going to go 'La la la la la la, life is full of cappuccino, cappuccino. La la la la la la, ha ha ha ha ha. We're having a lot of fun. Lovely lights, lovely lights, lovely lights. Fun, fun, fun, fun, fun.' [*Laughter*]

And he comes back with the shelving going, 'Honey, honey, honey, there's people out there having a much better life than us. What are we going to do? I think we've settled down too early.' 'Ah, just put the shelving up. You'll be fine.' 'Sure, okay … [*Laughter*] 'Can I have another tranquillizer?

But it is a weird thing like. These people are just having a shit time as well. It's torrents of loneliness but I bet you there's some bloke, one bloke on his own, who's in the middle ground, who's found perfect happiness, kind of going, 'Fucking idiots … I'm not telling anyone the way forward though, fuck you all.'

I hope that's the case, you know.

'Cos like the thing is, I do think anyone here who's settled down in your lives, you know, it's brilliant. It's the most natural thing to share your life with someone you love and have a soul mate. But if there's anyone in this room who is settling for, you know, you're making a mockery of your lives and you don't deserve a life and I suggest you kill yourself. [*Laughter*].

But, I really do mean that you know, 'cos settling down is beautiful, settling *for* is atrocious.

Let's take the extreme example, battered wives. They look in the mirror, they see those bruises and they go, 'But he loves you.' No. He doesn't love you. He doesn't like you very much. In fact, he probably hates you. Surely you must realize there are millions of us out there who will never physically harm you, but will give you a life of *mental* torture. [*Laughter*]

Get out of that relationship. We're all out here, you know.' 'Honey, I will never hit you but I might not speak to you for a couple of weeks. 'Just fucking hit me, would you?' No. [*Laughter*] But I just want to point out one thing. Again, this is nothing that you're going to learn here, but it's something that we try not to remind ourselves of …

Sex is not spiritual, never was, never will be, stop kidding yourself that it is. No, I love sex. It's good fun, good exercise and a great way to meet people but it's not, [*Laughter*] it's not spiritual and stop pretending it is, because then every time you make love you have to make it special and sometimes it isn't and it fucking does your head in, okay? [*Laughter*]

And I remember the moment where this was clarified for me …

I was in this room and this woman was giving me a blowjob and in the exact same room there was a dog licking its balls, and I couldn't tell the difference in noise. [*Laughter*].

You're just hearing these thoughts, I'm living with them, folks, okay … It was an awkward time in my life, you know.

'Oh, yeah, that was great, do you want a biscuit? [*Audience applause*] Come on, we'll go for a quick walk …'

'Religion'

Oxford (1993),
Laughing Stock LAFFC 36

HUGHES

And it's brilliant, like Bishop Casey like,
you know, he slept with this woman, has a
kid, and then he gives her like £200,000,
like, to forget all about it, like, you
know. And it's brilliant in Ireland,
because the Church is always saying, do
this and do that. Now they can't anymore,
can they, like. You know, oh, because the
next time you go to confession, they say,
'Well, what are your sins?' You can go,
'Er, you go first, Father.'

[*Laughter*]

And of course the Catholic Church was
saying, look, come on, it was the heat of
the moment, right, he slept with this
woman, heat of the moment, and I've never
really understood what that meant like, you
know, no-one goes, [*Puffs*] 'Oh it's hot in
here isn't it? Let's fuck.'

[*Laughter*]

Never had that like. And how can it be heat
of the moment? The Bishop has about 60
different robes on like; he's not going to
go, 'Okay, I'll be with you in a minute.'

[*Laughter*]

'Oh, I'm gone all soft again now, gees.'

180

[*Laughter*]

But it must be great for the people of Galway to know every time they were putting money into the church collection they were helping put an American kid through college.

[*Laughter*]

I'd rather it go to a little kid like.

Well, I've given money to the Church before; I'm going to ring up that little kid in America and say, 'Are you doing your homework?'

[*Laughter*]

'Make sure you do now okay? I'm looking after you; I'm your sponsor.'

Yeah well I go to church once a year. Any Catholics in tonight? The just-in-case brigade?

[*Laughter*]

The Christmas Eve, half-eleven, bit pissed, midnight mass, could be a laugh once?

[*Laughter*]

'Excuse me mate, I haven't been to one of these dos for ages, what's the deal here?'

[*Laughter*]

We're celebrating Christ's birthday. Oh, gees. Happy birthday to you.

[*Laughter*]

Happy birthday. Has he turned up yet? Oh, acting cool. Is he late again? [*Laughing*] He's got a life, I suppose. [*Laughs*]

Doubt it.

[*Laughter*]

No, I go to church once a year, but I used to go in April, on a Tuesday, because then it's just usually me and the priest, and there's a fair chance of a shag that way like, you know.

[*Laughter*]

Oh come on, it's very romantic, isn't it? Wine, candles, he's wearing a lovely dress. Good night out.

[*Laughter and applause*]

Oh strike me down now. Come on. Proof. Yeah, it would be so funny if a bolt of lightning came in, hey?

[*Laughter*]

Fuck, there is a God. I'm out of here.

[*Laughter*]

Going to church. Yeah, no, it's pathetic really. And also like, I'm not knocking anyone's faith, because everyone's faith is very important, but that doesn't seem to be enough for certain people. Certain fundamentalists want everyone to believe, because you go, 'Well I don't believe,' and they go, 'Well you have to.'

[*Laughter*]

Well surely it's enough that you believe, that's enough. 'No, no, you have to read it as well. Have you not read the Bible?' I says, 'Yeah, and have you read Helter Skelter?'

[*Laughter*]

Swamped for a little bit there like, you know. Like if the priests changed the rules a bit, they could actually relate to something to our lives in church. Because you go every week, and he goes, 'And now we have St Paul's third letter to the Corinthians,' and you're thinking, 'Well why don't these guys ever write back for a start, like you know?' Not exactly the best pen pals in the world, are they?

St Paul every day with the postman, 'Hi, anything for me? I'll be in here writing another letter. I did put the self-addressed envelope in.'

[*Laughter*]

Just once I'd like to go to the church, and the priest goes, 'We have a post card here from the Corinthians.'

[*Laughter*]

'Oh look, Jerusalem at night …'

[*Laughter and applause*]

'Thanks for the letter, Paul, from all the Corinthians. We've moved. No forwarding address. Okay. Let's get on with the ceremony.'

We're going to have an interval in a couple
of minutes, you know, so you can have a
beer and an ice cream and Steve will
probably move a couple of rows back.

[*Laughter*]

But you're having a good time, Stevie? [*to
a man in the audience who is a school
teacher*]

[*Laughter*]

Yeah, don't bother asking me, Steve, oh no.
All one way with you isn't it, oh yeah?

[*Laughter*]

Sean how are yourself, sir, young fellow?
Oh no, none of that like, you know. I
suppose I have to call you 'Sir' later on.
And have you got control over your class
when you're teaching? You have?

STEVE

Yes.

[*Laughter*]

HUGHES

I don't ever doubt it. You have that look.
Unless you've got one of those faces,
because you look kind of gentle and nice,
do you have one of those horrible stares
that says like, 'Did you do your homework?'

[*Laughter*].

He's carrying a gun, I'm sure of it.

[*Laughter*]

You learn how to lie in school as well. Why is it as well that teachers say, 'Why were you late this morning?' And you know what we do: we just make up one of those excuses. Like, which one do you want? The car broke down? The bus was late? And teacher goes, fair enough, have a note to that effect tomorrow, like, you know. I'd like to see a kid go into the classroom, and you go, 'Why were you late this morning?' And he goes, 'Well I thought, double maths this morning, fuck it, I'll have a lie in.'

[*Laughter*]

All right, Stevie ?

[*Laughs*].

And do they have to call you Mr ah, what's your full name? Mr Maughn. Imagine what your nickname was.

[*Laughs*]

'Here's Mr Sad Face.'

[*Laughter*]

And do you make them, are you one of the liberal teachers who says, 'Hey, call me Steve?' No.

It's Mr Maughn, yeah? Call me Mr Maughn.

[*Laughter*]

People are so cynical about school as well, because you learn how to read and write at school, thanks to people like you Mr Maughn.

Because no, actually I'm with you all the
way, because like teachers get paid
terribly and it is a hard job, because it
is all about confidence as well, like you
have to like pretend you're quite tough
like, you know. Because we had a teacher in
our class, Mr Shaw, and he used to teach us
science, and he had no control over the
class.

And he'd go, 'Don't do that. Much.'

[*Laughter*]

Our homework of a night, was to try and
give Mr Shaw a nervous breakdown. That was
the basic deal, yeah. Mr Shaw would walk
into the classroom; we'd all start swaying,

[*Laughter*]

'Boys, stop that swaying over there.'

'We're not swaying, sir'

[*Laughter*]

'Sir, I think you're having that breakdown
you've been worried about.'

[*Laughter*]

At the end of the class he'd go, 'Any
questions?'

'Yeah, Mr Shaw, um, why aren't you
married?'

[*Laughter*]

'Huh?'

[*Laughter*]

No, because, that's the only thing I, I, I
despised about going to school is that the
teachers destroyed poetry for me. You know
what I'm talking about, because when you
read a poem, you kind of read the poem, and
you kind of, you say, oh, I like that, and
you kind of get into it and stuff, and then
the teacher says, 'What do you think that's
about?', and you think, well, like you
know, I really like that imagery, and I
think that's what it's about. And they go,
'Well it isn't, okay?'

[*Laughter*]

'It's about the Russian revolution, okay?
What's this about *daffodils* and shit? It's
the Russian revolution, okay.'

[*Laughter*]

So don't do those things will you, Steve.
No, you just do what you want, Steve;
you're a lot bigger than me as well.

So, um, we'll have a little break now,
yeah?

'Nightclubs'

Glasgow (1996),
Laughing Stock LAFFC 57

Bouncers, they're a weird breed, aren't they? Do you think when they row with their wife, they probably never shout.

They just go, 'Look, I'm afraid I'm going to have to ask you to leave. The relationship is over.'

[*Laughter*]

And, like, what's this music they're playing now? Ah-ah-ah-ah-ah-ah-ah, I love this mix, ah-ah-ah-ah.

[*Laughter*]

People who go to nightclubs are people who can't get sex and want to simulate it for six hours, you know? [*Laughter*] You're not turning anyone on there, like, you know? This music, ah-ah-ah-ah-ah-ah, that's not music. That's a taxi driver outside beeping his horn. Who ordered this? Ah-ah-ah. DJ's going, this'll save me a fortune. Put your headlights on.

[*Laughter*]

I'm probably just jealous because I could never dance, even when I was a teenager. Dad was embarrassed collecting me from the disco.

[*Laughter*]

'But, dad, I'm having fun.'

And the clothes these kids are wearing. They wear all that baggy stuff. You know, what's the deal here? Have I missed the whole culture thing?

[*Laughter*]

'Come on, the six of us, let's all just walk around like …'

[*Laughter*]

And they wear those hats as well and I don't know why. Somebody is … like *The Face* … I blame *The Face* for this as well, because this … [*Puts on baseball cap*] these do not look cool.

[*Cheering, applause*]

Rap people wear these as well and they have those tough names as well. Ice-T, don't dis with me, okay? [*Laughter*] Or I'll set my friend on you, Snoop Doggy Dog. [*Laughter*]

[*Barking noise*] They're making up their own language now as well. Don't dis with me or I'll buck you in the head.

[*Laughter*]

'Excuse me, Mr Ice, when … when you're bucking me in … in the head, will that be a good thing or a bad thing? I'd like to … will I be in pain or will I have pleasure? Could you clear that up for me?' You're dissing my brother and you're dissing my sister and if you do the washing up use disinfectant.'

[*Laughter*]

The weird thing about wearing a hat as well is that for the next two hours you still have the sensation that you're wearing a hat.

[*Laughter*]

Walking around the street going, 'Have I got a hat on?' I think I've got a hat on. 'Excuse me, passer-by, have I got a hat on?'

So what do you think the deal is with all these guys with the baggy clothes? Do you think they've all got very fat older brothers at home who give them hand-me-downs?

[*Laughter*]

'Hey, brother, I'm too obese to leave the house. You can have me clothes.'

[*Laughter*]

If you're driving home tonight and you see one of those guys with the caps on, beep your horn. I guarantee you they'll start dancing.

[*Laughter*]

Or buck you in the head.

10. EDDIE IZZARD

Squirrel with a gun

If Eddie Izzard was an animal what would he be? A cat. A possum? A ring-tailed lemur? I'd put my money on a shark. Think of Eddie on stage, he's always moving, always gliding purposefully towards something. And think of Eddie off stage. Once again, he's always moving, never staying in one place for too long. Yes, a shark. That's it.

The Yemen-born comedian is conclusive proof that, if you've got talent and you stick at it, sooner or later everyone will catch on. He certainly wasn't an overnight success. After a spell in a double act and as a street entertainer, Izzard wasn't put off by universal displays of disaffection. For the first part of his comedy career he might as well have had yellow bollards positioned all around him and a ribbon of tape declaring 'talent-free zone'. Others might have given up. Not Izzard. If they didn't get him, that just made him try harder.

In the late eighties, he concentrated on the stand-up comedy circuit, developing his groovy chatterbox stream-of-consciousness style. Ben Elton and Harry Enfield were the hottest comedians at the time. Thatcher-bashing and the social comment of Loadsamoney was in, freewheeling sur-realism was out. Not that this put Izzard off. Slowly but surely things fell into place. People seemed to understand that this person on stage was actually funny.

The real turning point was taking the ultimate small busi-nessman step and setting up his own club, Raging Bull, first in

Soho and then at the Shaw Theatre in Euston. It might have been the last roll of the dice for Eddie's comedy career but it worked. The loose, late-night ambience and the opportunity to spool out ideas without being wrenched offstage by an irate promoter was the real answer to his problems. The atmosphere was more relaxed, more conducive to creativity. Or as Izzard called it, 'talking bollocks'. The audiences were more open-minded. Gigs got better, crowds got more appreciative. It didn't even matter that he lost £10,000. He'd thrown the comedic equivalent of a double six and was up and running.

By 1991, Izzard was the most talked about act on the British circuit. When he was shortlisted for the Perrier Award alongside Frank Skinner, Jack Dee and Lily Savage (the loud-mouthed alter ago of Paul O'Grady) at that summer's Edinburgh Fringe Festival, no-one was surprised. Skinner won, but this was easily the strongest shortlist in the Award's ten-year history. In any other year Izzard would have romped to victory.

With most comics one can easily play spot-the-influence, but what made Izzard so refreshing was that he seemed to come out of no tradition whatsoever. Of course, he was a mad fan of the Goons – he had listened to them on Radio Dubai when his father worked for BP in the Middle East in the sixties. Of course he had swallowed Monty Python hook, line and sinker. But Izzard wasn't just repackaging lunatic comedy for the alternative age. There were all sorts of other ideas floating about under that thatch of blonde hair. He had clearly spent more time than was healthy watching cable channel documentaries about such subjects as Greek mythology, the Napoleonic wars and the Nazi Party. He was very big on getting his information from moving pictures: 'I'm not widely read,' he explained, 'I'm thinly read.'

And he clearly had a thing about voices too. Even though the only impression he could ever do well was James Mason, who became a regular character in his flights of fancy, either knocking around with his mate Sean Connery, or playing

God rushing everywhere with soot and jam trying to make the world on time. You never knew quite what you were going to get though – and neither did Izzard, since nothing was ever written down. He grandly suggested this was because he was part of an ancient, longstanding tradition of oral storytelling, though the fact that he was partially dyslexic and wrote very slowly might have had something to do with it too.

And then, of course, there was the anthropomorphism – ascribing human characteristics to animals. In the sketch featured here, dating from the mid-nineties, Izzard delivers the definitive riff on the difference between cats and dogs. Comedians have done this sort of thing a thousand times, but no-one has captured the dumb benevolence of dogs and the slightly sinister nature of cats quite as well as this. He paints a beautiful picture of life at home with a dog taking your blood pressure while your cat is drilling behind the sofa: 'They've got goggles on, it's OK.'

Like a mutant hybrid of David Attenborough's *Life on Earth* and Spike Milligan's *Q* (curious fact: Spike Milligan was stationed in Izzard's adolescent hometown of Bexhill-on-Sea during World War II) the animal kingdom meandered in and out of Izzard's stage shows. His first routine that really captured the public's attention was his story about learning French at school and the weird phrases that the teachers taught him, such as, '*Le singe est dans l'arbre*' ('the monkey is in the tree'). When would one ever be likely to need to use that phrase, he asked. He even considered the possibility of purposely taking a monkey across the Channel with him on holiday and pushing it up a tree just so that he could say it.

Post-Perrier the natural next step would normally be to capitalize on media interest and spread yourself all over the television screen, but Izzard had other ideas. He decided to decline the inevitable offers from the box. Keep 'em keen, treat 'em mean. Less is more. Instead he decided to make up for the years when he couldn't get people to listen by touring extensively and showing the world that he could do it. It was a bold, brave move that went against contemporary business models, since it was usually television that raised a performer's profile and enabled them to sell tickets. The closest precedent, if there was any at all, was Billy Connolly, whose act was too raw to be contained on the small screen.

The tactic seemed to work. In February 1993, Izzard opened at the Ambassador's Theatre in London. His one-month run sold out and was extended. In the end Izzard played there for three months, picking up rave reviews and an Olivier Award nomination. Looking back on the show now, it's remarkable how prescient parts of it are. Between the familiar riffs on Star Trek and clammy weather being the worst kind of weather, there's a piece on the London bombings of the time which would have worked just as well post 7/7 – how when there's a terrorist alert dogged London commuters just get on with their lives and devise a different route into work.

You wouldn't really put him down as a topical or a political comedian but the most unlikely current events can prompt some brilliantly offbeat thoughts. Speaking after an incident when someone had fired a starting pistol at Prince Charles, he wondered what their motives had been: 'You can't start someone to death.' Freud, however, would surely have a field mouse, er, day, with Izzard's onstage leaps of the imagination and word association games.

Television eventually tempted him, but inevitably he did it strictly on his terms. He wrote, but didn't appear in, the Channel 4 sitcom pilot *Cows*. This was a completely conventional sitcom about a classic dysfunctional family called the Johnsons. So far, so sitcom, except that the family was dressed in cow costumes. The closest comparison was Glen Larson, whose Far Side cartoons imagined the inner thoughts of animals as if they were humans too. The sitcom didn't quite work. Maybe it needed an appearance from Izzard himself, who always magically brought any off-kilter idea to life on stage. Take his thoughts on the behaviour of squirrels who have a funny habit of halting, dead in their tracks for no apparent reason: 'And sometimes they stop, as if to say, "Did I leave the gas on?" No! No. I'm a fucking squirrel.'

As Izzard's career took off, he broke a new piece of news to his fans: he was a transvestite. No-one was particularly shocked. It didn't lose him any support. In fact it may have gained him some. The only people who seemed to have difficulties were the gangs of meatheads who yelled at him in the street: 'They hang around in groups of five because they have a fifth of a personality each.'

Izzard did have to explain to the press ad nauseam that he was not gay, but a heterosexual man who liked to wear women's clothing. Over the years, he came up with various explanations to stop himself from being bored with talking about the subject. His initial stance was that he was standing up for 'total clothing rights'. Nobody bats an eyelid when women wear trouser-suits so why shouldn't he wear off-the-shoulder numbers, mandarin dresses or La Perla underwear. Depending on what mood he was in, Eddie might be wearing either just a hint of lipgloss and nail polish or the full monty. It was his right to choose.

Izzard's mother Ella (he named his company, Ella Communications after her) died of cancer when he was six. But, while he suggests that maybe he got into live performance for a 'surrogate affection thing', he does not think that her death – though traumatic for him – has anything to do with his interest in women's clothes. That, he maintains, is purely to do with something buried deep within his genetic make-up.

Over the years, he modified his position a little. He was the world's first 'action transvestite', able to leap tall buildings in a single bound and not get a ladder in his tights. Then there was his idea that he was a 'male tomboy' or a 'straight lesbian', which kind of made sense. More recently he came up with a new definition which was maybe the best one of all:

'I'm all boy, plus extra girl.' Lucky Eddie. He has done his best, however, to keep the subject separate from his comedy career – not an easy thing when you come onstage sporting stilettos, a basque and false rubber 36DD breasts based on Uma Thurman's boobs. As I said, lucky Eddie.

If television was a difficult medium for him, he had no such problems with his live performances. Over the years the theatres got bigger and the runs longer. He had complete mastery of his audience from opening to encore. By the end of the nineties he had taken stand-up comedy out of theatres and into arenas. He wasn't the first one to do this, but he was arguably the first one to do it on a regular basis, touring arenas all over the country rather than playing one-offs in selected venues.

In 2005, for instance, Lee Evans claimed the record for playing to the largest comedy audience when he appeared in front of 10,108 fans at Wembley Arena in December 2005. Evans' impressive achievement was ratified by the *Guinness Book of Records*. But Izzard had claimed to have played to an unofficial audience of 13,632 at the Manchester Evening News Arena two years earlier on his Sexie tour. Not bad for a bloke in a frock talking bollocks.

By this time Izzard wasn't just known for his stand-up comedy. He had also carved out a career as a stage actor. Part of his strategy as a comedian was to make his name so that he had the muscle to land decent roles. It seemed to be paying off handsomely when he co-starred in David Mamet's cerebral drama *The Cryptogram* in 1994. In 1999, he was perfectly cast as controversial comic icon Lenny Bruce in a revival of the 1970 play *Lenny*. Izzard put in a memorable performance as the troubled comic. A West End production of *A Day in the Death of Joe Egg* followed, taking Izzard to Broadway in 2003, where his performance earned him a Tony Award nomination. Izzard has made more inroads into America than any comedian of his generation, boasting sell-out American runs and a prestigious HBO special – in 2000, the television version of the Dress to Kill show picked up two Emmys for performance and writing, which was ironic for a gig that was never written down. (His celebrated animal line 'We wanted diamonds, or sherbet or a squirrel with a gun!' originates from the Dress to Kill tour.)

His movie career has been slightly more problematic. He has had no shortage of parts, but has yet to land a defining role that could put him in the frame for major leads. He has had brief turns in everything from *Velvet Goldmine,* to *The Avengers,* to *Ocean's Twelve.* He played a cowboy opposite Michael Madsen in the movie *Blueberry* directed by France-based auteur Jan Kounen, which he memorably described as a 'baguette-y western'.

But his most notable role to date is playing Charlie Chaplin in Peter Bogdanovich's murder mystery *The Cat's Meow.* Izzard has been upfront about admitting that cinema is his ultimate goal, describing his comedy career to the *Observer*'s Geraldine Bedell in 2004 as 'a big curvy route to get into films'.

There's a part of me that hopes Izzard will succeed as an actor, but also a part of me that hopes he will not. It would be a great shame if Hollywood permanently lured him away from stand-up. Izzard remains a unique talent. Since he first made his name, there have been plenty of acts who have tried their hand at his spontaneous freeform yarn-spinning. When Alan Davies first emerged, if you closed your eyes he sounded like an Eddie Izzard tribute act. Ross Noble is certainly another consummate exponent of freewheeling fun, but there are few others who do flights of fancy quite as wonderfully as Izzard.

This kind of improvisation is a comedy muscle that needs to be kept in shape. I've seen a lot of show-stopping Izzard performances where he has effortlessly spun words in the air like a verbal juggler, but I did see one very ropy gig when he played a West End benefit for Edinburgh's Gilded Balloon venue, which had been destroyed in a fire. Izzard came on stage, did his usual ums and aahs, but never stopped umming and aahing, and failed to hit his stride. By his own admission, he was on the rusty side, because he had been too busy working on other projects to be fully match-fit.

The difficulty is finding time for comedy in an increasingly busy schedule. If it isn't Hollywood making demands on Izzard's time, it is Europe. He is a passionate advocate of all things continental, publicly campaigning for the Euro and doing his bit for Federalism. 'I grew up in Europe,' he told his San Franciscan audience during his American Dress to Kill Tour 'where history comes from.' He has done gigs in France in French, and hasn't ruled out more political involvement in the future, possibly, even, standing for election as a Member of the European Parliament. Now Izzard making his maiden speech is a gig I would really love to see. You'd probably need to be a shark to negotiate those treacherous political waters, so maybe he is eminently qualified.

Bruce Dessau

'Advertising'

Albery Theatre, London (1995),
Laughing Stock LAFFCD 38

You know, some people are widely read. I'm thinly read. I've read fuck all

[*Laughter*]

I'm very proud of it. There are certain people who say, 'I've read Dr Banofsky's book on cat eating by Mahaba …' You know I just haven't read anything, because I'm partially dyslexic. I was fully dyslexic until I met someone who was more dyslexic than me and they said you're only partially dyslexic.

There's a lot of rivalry in the dyslexic camp.

[*Laughter*]

Rivalry with three Vs …

Yeah. So anyway, advertising, yes, that's what I brought you here to talk about. Yes. Advertising. Because I've been looking at it and I've noticed that certain people in the advertising area get paid huge wodges of cash in brown paper bags in order to subtly adjust our minds. Because, like in the old days, adverts, perhaps before the 50s, I don't know, adverts were much more blatant. Adverts were much more, 'Come on, there it is, come on, don't look at it all day, there it is.'

[*Laughter*]

And as consumers, we were much more, oh
okay, fine, I didn't realize …

[*Laughter*]

But nowadays we have choice, don't we?
We're much more choosy and we're much more
aware of what we can buy, so the adverts
are more subtle, they're more soft sell.
Adverts are much more like … [*Gentle
humming of ad style music*]

[*Laughter*]

[*Humming gets louder*] Oh, look at that,
those two people like it.

[*Laughter*]

And they're shagging!

[*Laughter and applause*]

And that's what happens, isn't it? Shagging
sells everything.

There's that advert for coffee: 'You coming
round for a cup of coffee? OK, let's shag.'

[*Laughter*]

And that advert for chocolate bars. Two
bits of chocolate bar, one eats one, one
eats the other. 'Oh let's have a shag.'

[*Laughter*]

That cleaning stuff, cleans the floor,
clean the floor clean, and then you can
shag on the floor.

[*Laughter*]

Now the washing area, washing powder,
washing clothes, laundry, all that kind of
stuff, that's a very advertising-led area,
where there's a huge amount of advertising
saying, wash your clothes, wash your
clothes. Or no-one will shag you.

[*Laughter*]

And I think, if there wasn't all the
advertising, we probably wouldn't wash,
we'd just spray our clothes and say oh that
smells okay, now …

And it's quite a ceremony. Washing your
clothes, you can take it down to the
laundrette, that's one way. You get a bag,
it's easy, three months worth of washing
into a huge bag and drag it down to the
laundrette, wearing clothes that should be
in the bag really.

[*Laughter*]

That's why you've gone to the laundrette
because you've got nothing left to wear.
You're wearing your dressing gown to work
and stuff like that … So, you throw it all
into the wash, and you've got big machines
down the laundrette, huge machines with big
porthole windows and you shove it all in.
Never separate out at the laundrette. Shove
it all in …

[*Laughter*]

And you've got one choice: Bizarre Wash.

[*Laughter*]

And you always have to sacrifice a few socks and a pair of pants to the God of Laundrettes … who lives at the back of the machines with chopsticks … 'Oh lovely, thank you, yes. Bit of fabric softener?

[*Laughter*]

And you take your washing out, shove it into a tumble dryer, and the tumble dryer glues it together with static electricity.

[*Laughter*]

So that you can get the washing out, put it on your head and walk out.

[*Laughter*]

Next day you put on a pair of socks and the rest of the washing shouts, 'We're coming too, we're coming too … '

'Piss off, I'm just wearing these now …'

[*Laughter*]

You're trying to chat someone up. 'Yeah, no, I agree with you.' 'Piss off.

'Sorry, I don't know whose it is, it's stray, stray washing … '

[*Laughter*]

Or you can wash your clothes at home. And at home in people's flats and houses, they have a machine with a huge dial with all the letters of the alphabet on … And no instructions.

[*Laughter*]

You've just got to guess. You'll say, well
I think I'll have an 'H' wash. Get some
powder and you stuff it all in, and
invariably you get the stuff going, and a
pair of socks come in late. 'Sorry we're
late, sorry …'

[*Laughter*]

'We were lying in the dust where you left
us … Oh, has the programme started?

And then you let the socks into the
washing, and the socks are going, 'Excuse
me, pardon me, sorry.'

[*Laughter*]

'We're supposed to be here. We've got
tickets.'

Or you do a whites clothing wash. You say
I'll wash all my white clothes, and you
shove all your whites down in a big pile,
and you put some clothes in there which are
almost white, and then you think no, and
you take them out, push them to one side.

Then you shove it all in. And ah, the rest
of the deeper-coloured clothes say, 'Oh,
he's doing a whites wash first …

And they go: 'Okay, blue underpants, you
will infiltrate whites wash … You are our
best undercover clothing.'

[*Laughter*]

'We've done you some forged papers. You will be disguised as a white handkerchief, okay?'

[*Laughter*]

'These have been done up by Donald Pleasence and will be good. I believe you've been practising a white handkerchief accent?' 'Yes, I have, yes I have.'

[*Laughter*]

'Very good. Now off you go.'

Blue underpants goes off, sneaks inside the white wash, usually inside a shirt. Shirts are a bit dopey, aren't they?

[*Laughter*]

And it gets in, and white wash goes in, and soon as the clothing starts going around in the wash, blue underpants comes up the window and goes, 'Hello, hello, blue pants here. Blue pants in a white wash.'

Get the blue pants out!

'It's an emergency, break glass, smash glass!'

[*Laughter*]

And blue pants are going 'I'm draining, I'm draining …' And if all your clothes came out blue, it'd be fine, wouldn't it? But your clothes tend to come out a colour that's called pants left in wash.

[*Laughter*]

And people know, and they point, going
yeeah, yeeah, and then they stab you.

[*Laughter*]

Well, apparently sometimes, you know.

So, this is it, so these adverts … Nowadays
we're more sophisticated as consumers. We
go into supermarkets. We read the labels.
This jam was made by Nazis with dead twigs,
bits of mud and spit.

[*Laughter*]

'No, I don't think I'll have that one.'

[*Laughter*]

This jam is made by groovy people, out of
fruit that agreed to be in the jam in the
first place. Volunteer fruit.

[*Laughter*]

Also known as free-range fruit … Allowed to
casually chat to chickens …

[*Laughter*]

You know, chickens, free-range chickens are
so pushy, aren't they? They go, 'Ah yes,
all this field will be range free now. And
then we've got the next field, we'll range
free there.'

[*Laughter*]

'And the big house at the back, we'll knock
that down.'

'The farmhouse, yeah, we'll knock that
down.'

[*Laughter*]

'And that's our Range Rover, over there.'

[*Laughter*]

Have you ever seen that? Those Range Rovers, with very high seats and chickens driving along?

[*Laughter*]

Yes, so anyway, we are more sophisticated, and the adverts are generally more sophisticated. We have stories and graphics and cryptic adverts where you have to work out what they're talking about. Then you go, 'Oh, I see,' then you don't buy it.

[*Laughter*]

But not the washing powder people. They've done the research; they've come to the conclusion that everyone prefers this bloke with the clipboard thing. This, this has been going since the fifties, someone who's locked in the supermarket going, 'Are you happy with your wash? Excuse me, are you happy with your wash?'

[*Laughter*]

Or out on motorways … 'Are you happy with your wash?' [*Makes sound of car speeding past*]

[*Laughter*]

'Tell me, are you happy with your wash?' [*Sound of car speeding past*]

[*Laughter*]

Small dog, 'Are you happy with your wash?'

[*Laughter*]

'I'm a dog.'

[*Laughter*]

'I don't know.'

'The Queen'

Hammersmith Apollo, London (1997),
Laughing Stock LAFFCD 65

We have a Queen. We have a queen bee. Um …
still in this country the monarchy is
fighting for its life because … well the
Queen has got this thing that … the old
lady thing … she does live forever. The
Queen is just there, boom, boom, boom …

[*Laughter*]

Yes, so the Queen is sooo severe; the Queen
is too ooooh. And her glasses are getting
bigger and bigger and bigger. She's
becoming an owl. [*Laughter*] Queen Owl. One
day her glasses will be bigger than her
body and she will light many fires when the
sun shines down …

[*Laughter*]

And oh yes, Diana died. Diana died and
everyone was thrown by this. And the
audience goes very quiet when I talk about
this. [*Loud laughter*] No there's no big
jokes about death, you know. She died, and
everyone was thrown. I mean, I wasn't a big
fan. I didn't really dislike her. I
preferred Diana's route to the Queen's
route though because the Queen was going
'ummm' [*Deep pitch*], and Diana was slightly
more 'ummm' [*Higher pitch*]. [*Laughter*]
That's the tonality of their direction. I
don't know what I'm talking about, but you

know what I mean. You know exactly what I mean. No. OK.

Anyway, she died and yeah, I think the death … it threw us because it was like a soap opera. Every day, front page news. Diana, Dodi Al Fayed … on a holiday, on another holiday, on a second holiday, on a fifteenth holiday, in a boat, on a boat, near a boat …

[*Laughter*]

And then dying in the middle of the night, you know, vroom, in a bizarre kind of spy story type of thing. And it was like something from the *X Files*.

I mean, I really like it. You see it. It's front page; Scully, Mulder, Scully, Mulder. She's wearing no clothes, he's wearing some clothes. [*Laughter*] She's wearing very little clothes in a lot of photos isn't she? Oh Yes.

[*Laughter*]

I noticed the lack of clothing that started appearing round her. And she's sexy in that kind of very, tight, bob haircut type sexy way. Look Mulder, don't you get … She keeps being sceptical: 'This is it. I don't believe that Martians have taken over Kent.'

[*Laughter*]

'But they have Scully, they have. They've been there for six years. They've always been there forever. We've got a lot of files of it in the FBI. Haven't you read them?'

'No, I'm a doctor.'

[*Laughter*]

But imagine them. If that goes on, that sort of series you expect to go on and on. Imagine an episode coming out, 2 am in the morning on a Monday and they just killed off the characters and that was it: end of thing. And you'd go, eh?

[*Laughter*]

I was watching that …

[*Loud laughter and applause*]

So it's a kind of … I was watching that. We were following the story, and it's like some … it's a soap opera. And people send messages. You know, Tony Blair saying … coming on telly and Bill Clinton, and people saying, oh, we're sorry about this.

But the Queen said nothing, nothing. Monday nothing; Tuesday, Wednesday nothing; Thursday nothing. Friday it was as if someone was just pushing her in front of a television camera.

[*Laughter*]

'What? But I'm on holiday.'

[*Laughter*]

'Is it Christmas already?'

[*Loud laughter and applause*]

It was as if Charles was saying, 'Go on, get out there.'

'But do I have to? I'm in Scotland at the moment.'

And the trouble is the Queen can't talk from her heart. We have developed a sensibility in the 1990s of people going on telly and saying, 'Look, I feel this. I think that's wrong; I think that's right. This is how I feel about it.' And you try and talk from your heart, and people can sense it. But the Queen hasn't got that. She's got this 1950s thing of, I am very sorry about what has happened. Diana died and it's all very sad. You know, and you just think, oh, it's fluff, you know? I'd have more respect for her if she came out and said 'Look, Diana died. She was going in a different direction to me. We didn't get on very well, you know? But I didn't want her to die. I didn't want her to d–d–die.'

[*Laughter*]

As long as she doesn't stay on the 'D' too many times. 'I didn't want her to die.' I mean if she just was honest and open about it, because we know they didn't get on. There must have been fights going on, but she won't say that.

I'd also have more respect for the Queen if she said, 'I'm never going to resign. I'm going to stay here,' because that's what she wants to do. 'You know, I'm fucking holding on.'

[*Laughter*]

'I've super-glued the crown on. I'm travelling with this throne attached now. So you can all fuck off.'

[*Laughter*]

She's not going to resign. She's going to stay there. You can see the look in her eyes, in those big owl eyes. She's staying forever. The Queen's going for Queen Victoria's record. Queen Victoria was queen for 20,000 years.

[*Laughter*]

But in the fifties she was quite sexy. The Queen was quite sexy in a kind of not terribly sexy kind of way, but in a … use your imagination, you can probably get there, type of way.

[*Laughter*]

Fancy the Queen. Got a picture up behind the locker door. Fancy her. Shag the Queen.

[*Laughter*]

It could have happened … In the sixties London and Britain was hip for the first time since the Civil War. And the Queen should have gone with it …

Hip London, the Queen should have been in short skirts and an E-type jag, with a cigarette. [*Makes engine noise*]

[*Laughter*]

Margaret was getting there but … Police
going, 'Oi, you're speeding lady … '

'Fuck off, I'm the Queen.'

[*Loud laughter*]

'Where to now Phil? Phil, read the map.
Jesus, read it the right way up for God's
sake.'

[*Laughter*]

Oh, actually one last thing I should say
about the Diana thing, which puts a little
perspective on it for me, was the … my dad
mentioned this to me … Because Diana died
and there were two kids, and one was 17 and
one was about 13. A lot of sympathy and
that's understandable. My mum died when I
was 6 and my brother was 8, and no-one gave
a shit.

[*Laughter*]

'Helen of Troy'

Hammersmith Apollo, London (1997),
Laughing Stock LAFFCD 65

Anyway, so yeah, years ago you had Helen of
Troy; who was actually Helen of Greece
lands.

And there was Prince Paris from Troy. And a
huge siege happened because Helen … she was
so gorgeous. And Paris obviously came over
to visit her one day and said, 'Queen
Helen, you are kind of sexy; let me kiss
you with tongues.' And she was impressed.
And next day she bunked off with him and
the Greeks were fucked off and they tore
over with boats. And the siege of Troy
began …

And all the great warriors came to the
siege. Agamemnon, famous warrior. Ajax,
famous toilet cleaner …

[*Laughter*]

And Achilles, immortal man … except he had
an Achilles heel.

The irony of it.

[*Laughter and applause*]

'What mum, you mean I'm called Achilles and
I have an Achilles heel? I'll be a laughing
stock.'

[*Laughter*]

Achilles must have gone into battle
dragging his heel behind him: '… Ay, ay,
fuck off, me heel, leave it alone.' And
Trojans were coming out with crabs and
lobsters. Crabs and lobsters: get the heel,
get the heel.

[*Laughter*]

No, no crabs and lobsters, no crabs and
lobsters. Aaghhh. Put it behind a brick.
Aaghhh.

[*Laughter*]

If I was Achilles I would have put my foot
in a fuck-off block of concrete. First
starter for ten. No-one would be … look,
block of concrete, ha, ha, ha! *Block of
concrete*, tooh, tooh, tooh.

'See these swords I hold? Brrrhh, brrrhh,
brrrhh, brrrhh, brrrhh. Stick them in my
body. No problem at all. Phwoom, wahoo,
wahoo.'

[*Laughter*]

Cut my head off: I still keep going. Ha,
ha, ha, ha.

But then Achilles would actually have a
maximum radius. He wouldn't actually be
able to walk anywhere because his foot's in
a block of concrete. 'Could you come over
here please? Could *you* come over here … ?
Hello, could you come over here please?
Damn. Could you come over here please? I've
got something to show you.'

[*Laughter*]

'Yes, it's in my hand. Yes, no, you're going to have to come over. Damn, damn!'

[*Laughter*]

You'd have to put wheels underneath the block of concrete. Hoo, hoo, hoo, hoo, hoo … [*High pitched*]

[*Laughter*]

Brrrhh, hoo, hoo, hoo, hoo, hoo… But we know that wheels don't work very well on trolleys …

[*Laughter and applause*]

Round and round in circles, trying to go hoo, hoo, hoo … Hang on a sec, hoo, hoo, hoo … brrrhh. Thanks for waiting. Hoo, hoo, hoo.

Much better would be a hovercraft bottom bit on. Whooooo… [*Laughter*] whooo, whoooooooooo, brrrhh. [*Laughter*] And after a hard day's fighting you could get home and change from blow to suck. Woooooh woooh

[*Laughter*]

'Mum, can you move the plug, it's stuck.' Whoooooooooo-oooooo. It's the noise of vacuuming; that's the best thing. The switching on and switching off. Whooooooooo-whoooooo. [*Pitch going down*] [*Laughter*]

Whoooooooom. [*Pitch going up*] And you're vacuuming along. Normally if you're vacuuming, you've got a good strong vacuum cleaner, that's good. And sometimes you hear that noise, cadugadugadugadugadug … and you say, 'Was that a bit of grit? Was that a bit of money? Or the treasure of the Sierra Madras.' And you've got to know. You've got to know. You tear open the dust bag. What's in it? Well it's a bit of grit. Damn.

[*Laughter*]

But the Hoovers are way better than those old-type non-motor cleaner hodedededas. They made a noise like hodedededa, hodedededa. [*Laughter*] They just had brushes and you had to push them over the … hodedededa, hodedededa. And the dust is going, 'What exactly are you trying to do?'

[*Laughter and applause*]

'Well we are trying to whisk you, whisk you into here.' 'But we're coming straight back down again.' [*Laughter*] 'Well I don't know about that you know. You know, I'm just a hodedededa.'

[*Laughter*]

So anyway, Achilles, remember him? He was there. And he had an Achilles heel but he died …

And the siege continued, ten years of siege. And then the Greeks finally made their master stroke, final end game play, where they built a huge fuck-off horse a hundred metres high, made of wood. And they sailed off in their ships saying, 'Bye, bye, we're going now. You've won, bye. We've left you a huge fuck-off horse. As per usual ... '

[*Laughter*]

'As you normally do in these situations. Hope you enjoy it.' What's the precedent for leaving a huge fuck-off horse? Normally, if you have ten years of failure you'd leave some dog pooh behind. 'This ... this is what we think of you.'

[*Laughter*]

'You bastards. Helen, you still in there? You bastards.' So the Greeks sailed off in their ships, and they sailed over the horizon. And it dips right down, and they sailed to where it dips down behind the horizon, where you can't see it, if you've ever been to the horizon.

[*Laughter*]

And all the Greeks just hid behind the horizon, or just below the horizon. [*Laughter*] And they could crawl along just below the level of the horizon. And so they could get a good look at the Trojans, they would stick fish on their helmets and they could jump up and ...

So, yes, anyway, they built the big fuck-off horse and the Trojans came out and said, 'Oh, a big fuck-off horse, just what we've *always* wanted.' 'Come on, drag her

in. Come on Tony, Simon … ' I don't know
what Trojan names are like.

[*Laughter*]

Anyway they should have checked because it
was a big hollow horse. They should have
done that tapping thing; tap, tap, tap,
tap, tap; tap, tap, tap, tap, tap; tap,
tap, tap, tap, tap. Ay, hang on. Tap, *tap,*
tap, tap, tap, tap, tap. 'This one's
hollow. Get it open.'

And inside there'd be a load of Greeks …
'Hello. Oh, have they all gone? Oh damn. No
we forgot to set an alarm because it hasn't
been invented.' [*Laughter*] 'We were just
cleaning up …'

Hodedededa, hodedededa, hodedededa.

[*Laughter*]

'Yeah, so you must be Trojans, right?'
'Well this is Agamemnon. I'm Ajax, and this
is Prince Philip of England.'

[*Laughter*]

'Don't say a bloody word, Phil. Do not say
a word.'

[*Laughter and clapping*]

Yeah …

'Cats and Dogs'

Albery Theatre, London (1994),
Laughing Stock LAFFCD 38

Cats and dogs are very interesting with human beings, because we have a pet relationship with them and we're the only animals that do this …

You know, giraffes don't have pet gazelles. [*Laughing*]

'Gazelle, go and run in Africa.'

No, they don't say that. We have pets because they lower our blood pressure. This is apparently official, yeah? They lower our blood pressure and I don't know quite how they do that. You sort of … you stroke them, you go to sleep, and while you're asleep the dog puts one of those big puffy things [*Laughter*] on your arm, ch-ch-ch-ch-ch-ch, sssss, ch-ch-ch-ch-ch-ch, sssss. It's 180 over 60. What does that mean?

'I don't know. I'm a dog.'

[*Laughter*]

Actually, when doctors do that, they take your blood pressure, they're not actually taking your blood pressure. They're just fucking around with this thing … [*Pumps up imaginary blood pressure gauge*]

They've actually got a jumping spider behind your back and that's what they're doing.

[*Laughter*]

Because I … because I saw one once. I said, 'You've got a jumping spider behind my back.' He said, 'Yeah, that's what we do. It's the jumping spider time.' It's true. Yeah, so anyway, that's what they do.

So the dog takes your blood pressure and you fall asleep and the cat drains all the blood from your body and sells it to one of those mobile blood banks.

[*Laughter*]

That's why sometimes you wake up feeling all anaemic and you see your cat and dog counting out fivers [*Laughter*] as the van pulls off. Have you ever had that? No?

Well, I don't know. They … they lower our blood pressure.

You stroke a dog. Dogs go 'Woo-ooh' and cats go … [*Purring sound*] because they're drilling, aren't they? That's what they're doing.

[*Laughter*]

They're drilling. They drill for gold. They drill for oil. They drill for anything just for the love of drilling. When they're behind your sofa, they're just drilling. [*Purring sound*]

[*Laughter*]

They've got goggles on. It's okay.

[*Laughter*]

221

And your friends come and say, 'I think your cat's drilling behind your sofa.' You go, 'I don't think so, that's … that's purring, that noise, isn't it?'

'Cat, are you drilling?'

And the cat hears this and whips off the goggles and says, 'No, no, no, no.'

[*Laughter*]

'Drilling? No, I'm a cat. How would I know how to drill? That's purring you're thinking of, that is, I'm having a good old purr back here.'

'Not drilling, no, no.'

'Okay.'

[*Purring sound*] [*Laughter*]

Sometimes they drill 40 … 40 to 50 feet, you know that, just for the hell of it.

Cats are much cooler than dogs though, aren't they? Cats have a scam going. You buy them food. They eat the food. They go away. That's the deal. You have no control over your cat. You can't say to your cat, 'Cat, heel, stay, wait, lie down, roll over,' because the cat will just be sitting there going, 'Interesting words.' [*Laughter*] 'Have you finished?'

While you're shouting all this at your cat, your dog's right next to you going … [*Laughter*] 'What the hell are you doing?'

'I'm talking to the cat.'

'Oh, sorry.'

You wouldn't even dream of training a cat.

'Cat, come for training. Now, stay, stay … hello, hello …' [*Laughter*] They just don't care. They just piss off.

And … dogs and cats eat dog and cat food and you do this new improved cat and dog food thing and I don't know how you tell whether cat and dog food is new improved. Do the humans go, 'Mm, lovely'?

[*Laughter*]

I mean, dogs just eat anything. Dogs go [*Singing*], whatever that is.

And you say, 'Oh, is that … is it new improved, does it taste good?' And dogs go, 'Ah … I don't know.'

[*Laughter*]

Oh, it's all over my shirt now. [*Laughter*] They just want to eat it whereas cats are *much* more choosy. Cats sort of look through the food.

'Okay, right, so this is…?'

[*Laughter*]

'New improved, is it really, is it really?'

[*Laughter*]

'Well, I'm going out …'

[*Laughter, applause*]

And they ... and they walk up to the cat door and they just stop at the cat door and turn around and go ... 'Keys?'

[*Laughter*]

Whereas your dog can't go out. Your dog goes, 'Oh, can I go out?' And you go, 'No, I'm ... I'm busy at the moment.'

'But the cat went out.'

'Yes.'

'And I can't go?'

'No, no. He has a cat door, you see.'

'Oh, and ... and why?'

'Well, I don't know, I have no idea.'

[*Laughter*]

Which was the first cat that persuaded a human to put a cat door in? [*Laughter*] I don't know. They just do. We throw sticks for dogs. That's the level we have dogs at. You'd never dream of throwing one for a cat. You throw sticks for dogs and dogs go, 'Oh, he's dropped his stick, better go and get that.'

[*Laughter*]

'Saw you dropped your stick there.'

[*Laughter*]

And they'll bring it back. And you throw it again ...

'Hang on ...'

[*Laughter*]

'Did you see me just bring that back?'

[*Laughter*]

'And then you … you dropped it again.'

[*Laughter*]

'This is very weird. I don't know what's going on here. Now hang onto it this time. I don't want to piss about all the time, you know. [*Laughter*] Do you think I enjoy this? Ha-ha-ha. Hey, don't fucking throw it again.'

[*Laughter*]

That's why the third time when they come back they won't give it to you. They go, 'No, no, you'll only drop it … '

[*Laughter, applause*]

11. GREG PROOPS

You couldn't make it up ...

American comedians have always had a soft spot for Britain. Bob Hope was born here and kept popping back. Jerry Lewis played the London Palladium with Dean Martin in the fifties. In the sixties, Lenny Bruce's potty-mouthed philosophizing caused outrage at Peter Cook's Establishment Club. In the late seventies, I can recall a weird semi-autobiographical BBC sitcom-slash-sketch show starring Kelly Monteith. Whatever happened to Kelly Monteith? Then after that I think we finally scared them off.

At least until the late eighties, when slowly but surely a wave of Americans started pitching up in British comedy clubs. Stealing our jobs, stealing our women and finally with Rich Hall in the guise of Otis Lee Crenshaw, stealing our Perrier Award in 2000.

One of the pioneers of this sharp-tongued invasion was Greg Proops. The San Franciscan gag-smith is best known for his snappy puncturing of life's ridiculousness, as well as his suit and tie, his Buddy Holly glasses, quiff and regular appearances on *Whose Line is It Anyway?*, the Channel 4 comedy show that took improvisation – turning up on stage with script, no gags, just surviving on your wits – into the mainstream.

When not doing stand-up or improvising all over America, Proops is busy notching up international Air Miles. I caught up with him in London where he was stopping over on the way to a well-earned break in Sicily. As ever, he was combining business with pleasure, doing the Wednesday night show with the Comedy Store Players, Britain's oldest improvisation team who started back in 1985. Back then, the line-up included Paul Merton, who still turns up when he can, and a pre-*Wayne's World* Mike Myers.

He kindly found time in his never-ending schedule to fill me in on his past and present, the American invasion and the history of modern improvisation. He is the perfect gent and the ideal person to provide a comedy overview. In his 25-year career shuttling across the Atlantic he has seen comedy's ups and downs from the inside out.

It all started for Proops on the West Coast of America. 'I was born in San Carlos in 1959 and moved to San Francisco when I was a teenager. It was while I was studying at the San Francisco State University that I started to do stand-up.' He had previously been doing lots of acting but immediately relished the freedom of getting up on a makeshift stage in the dormitory canteen and saying whatever he liked. 'It's easy at that age. You don't even think about whether you are funny, you just say anything that comes into your head.'

He doesn't subscribe to the theory that comedians are usually the bullied kids or geeks. 'The notion that comics are these guys and women that got their arses kicked, I find the opposite is true. Patton Oswalt, who plays the short guy in the sitcom *King of Queens,* was class president; Lily Tomlin was a cheerleader; I did all the plays and talent shows. Every comic I can think of was the leading light of their high school. They always seemed to be organizing drama groups, writing or starting the comedy nights. And I was 18, when I started, Tom Rhodes was 15, Ross Noble was 15, Bill Hicks was 13. You need balls to get up on stage at that age when no-one is laughing.'

Proops feels that he fits into the template of the snotty young kid who has the nerve to try anything: 'I thought I was funny and when a professional show asked audience members to come on stage I decided to have a go. That was the Faultline Improvisation group, which Mike McShane [from *Whose Line is It Anyway*] joined a couple of years later.'

He believes that San Francisco has a very specific sense of comedy. 'There is a certain type of San Francisco comedian. I guess Robin Williams is the big amplified version of it. The late Warren Thomas used to say that Robin was our Elvis. The typical San Francisco style is fast, surreal – I hate to use the word intellectual, it's a terrible word for comedy, but there's an intelligence there. It is different to New York or Los Angeles.'

Proops was cutting his teeth as a performer just as the new wave of British comedians – Mayall, Sayle and co. – were making their mark with non-sexist, non-racist material. The difference was that while the British club comedians were considered to be alternative, there was no such label for their American counterparts, even though Proops was just as politically correct. 'When I started out we didn't consider ourselves alternative, we were just trying to make good comedy.' He admired the comedy greats – Steve Martin, Richard Pryor and Robin Williams, but with a bit of geographical and critical distance could understand why British comedians were reacting more against the their own old guard. 'There has always been a tradition going back in America to Lenny Bruce and Mort Sahl, of going back to basics. It's like rock and roll, when it gets too big you have to go back to playing in shitty little rooms where the person is talking about what they feel.'

The West Coast city has regularly produced hip performers who have gone on to bigger things. 'Other comedians that have come out of the scene include Paula Poundstone and Jake Johanssen. Kevin Pollak [best known as the shortest suspect in *The Usual Suspects*] was a San Jose comic, which is a fine distinction. Janeane Garofalo [the deadpan comic best known as the office cynic in *The Larry Sanders Show*] and David Cross [from cult show *Mr Show*] aren't from there but they've spent time there. I guess what we all have in common is this lefty thing, "The man is a drag, we read, we get high and we do what we want." That's San Francisco comedy.'

A quarter of a century after Proops started getting paid for gigs the scene is still thriving, but it has had its highs and lows. 'In the late eighties when I was there it was huge, but by 1989 the clubs were starting to close down. There were ten full-time clubs within an hour's drive, now there are only two.' It was around that time that Proops heard about the British comedy boom. 'People told me about the Comedy Store and Malcolm Hardee's Tunnel Club. I was interested in finding out more.' He had always enjoyed British humour, having grown up on a diet of British comedy. Contrary to popular belief Americans were exposed to more than Benny Hill: 'Peter Sellers, Pete & Dud ... *Dave Allen at Large* and *The Two Ronnies* were always on TV when I was young.'

One of the catalysts for the influx of American comics into Britain was acidic satirist Will Durst, who had appeared at the Edinburgh Festival a couple of times and had dipped his toes in the London circuit. 'I knew Will from San Francisco and he'd told me about it,' recalls Proops. In 1989 Durst picked up a Perrier nomination and then Jimmy Tingle repeated the feat in 1990. Tingle had a particularly tart line in putting down British audiences, recalls Proops: 'He came on in Edinburgh and said "Good evening Glasgow" or "Hello Europe, didn't we beat you guys in a war?"'

Proops first came over to England in 1989 when he was invited to take part in *Whose Line is It Anyway?* Mike McShane had already joined *Whose Line* ... in 1988, when it started. The Friday night series became an immediate success. The producer Dan Patterson had seen improvisation in America and at the Comedy Store in London and found a brilliant way of putting it on television – inspired by the games done in the clubs.

The format has now become a comedy cliché, but at the time it was a blast of fresh air. Host Clive Anderson would get performers such as Josie Lawrence, Paul Merton and John

Sessions to create songs out of nothing and act out various mundane storylines in unlikely film genres, such as putting out the milk in the style of film noir, or making the bed in the style of horror films. A particular favourite was when someone would have to turn up as a weird guest at a party and the others have to work out their affliction.

The inclusion of Americans and Canadians who had more of a history of freeform comedy gave the series a boost and extended its shelf-life. Others that took part regularly were Bill Murray look-alike Colin Mochrie and pencil-necked Ryan Stiles. With them on board, the series ran for a decade, but that wasn't the end of the story. Cable channel Comedy Central had been airing it in America, and it had picked up a following over there, so they decided the make their own shows, building them around chunky sitcom star Drew Carey. Proops had worked with Carey already so found himself back on board again for another four years, during which time the show moved over to ABC and became a big Stateside hit. SF's very own Elvis, Robin Williams, was even a guest on it.

As the nineties began, the American invasion gathered pace. In 1990, Bill Hicks came over as part of a 'Stand-up America' package show. The floodgates were opening. Motormouth comic-with-attitude Denis Leary also toured Britain. A couple of years later Rich Hall took the same route. 'The British press was writing about him as if they had discovered him, but he'd always been a hero of mine in the States because he'd done *Saturday Night Live* and *Letterman*,' remembers Proops, who soon found himself providing references for the likes of Dave Fulton, recommending him to London clubs such as The Red Rose and the Comedy Store. In quick succession Tom Rhodes and Arj Barker (Perrier Best Newcomer, 1997) followed. In recent years, a whole new generation of American comics have been drawn to Edinburgh, most notably New Jersey uber-geek Demetri Martin, who won the Perrier Award in 2000.

Proops was an established face on the British scene by now and spent more and more time gigging there. He appeared on the Channel 4 comedy show Viva Cabaret and did the Edinburgh Fringe Festival almost every year in the nineties, picking up his own Perrier Award nomination in 1993. He thought he was a seasoned performer but Edinburgh was something else. After his first residency there, he was ready to handle anything. 'A guy had a heart attack at one show, at another gig I walked my entire audience into the gig upstairs where the Doug Anthony All-Stars were playing. It was a very cool year, anything goofy that could happen did happen.'

Proops slotted snugly into the British comedy environment. He didn't have to adapt his material at all. Shared television programmes and movies meant everyone spoke the same language and had the same references. The only difference was attitude. 'If anything I finally found a place where I was the optimistic happy one, where I wasn't the only one going, 'Everything sucks.' I was just one of a giant chorus saying, 'Everything sucks,' so there was a ready market for my brand of snotty cynicism.'

As well as breaking through in Britain, he was also becoming a globetrotter, gigging as far afield as New Zealand and Canada, where he was a hit at Montreal's Just For Laughs Festival – 'part-trade show, part-drunk fest'. As the American club circuit shrank, the international festival circuit kept expanding. In Australia he met singer Gloria Estefan, who explained to him that her wallaby had recently committed suicide. 'I had to keep a straight face and all I was thinking was, "How does a wallaby commit suicide?"' He got a fair bit of material out of that anecdote.

There are comedians who get into stand-up to open other doors – for example, Eddie Izzard and acting – and then there are comedians who get into stand-up for the love of stand-up: Proops definitely falls into the second category. Not that he isn't averse to doing the odd bit of acting. 'I usually get cast as the weird, obsessive guy, not too much of a stretch really.'

(Curious fact: in 2001 Proops won a Comedians Special edition of *The Weakest Link* on American television.)

One of his oddest jobs was opposite Pamela Anderson in the short-lived American series *Stripperella*. 'I played a mad scientist who would give her stuff to do, like Q in James Bond. Her character was not just a stripper, she was also a superhero. I can't think why it was cancelled.'

Proops really dirty little secret, however, is the voiceover game. He has made a tidy living on the side from his trademark adenoidal patter. In *Star Wars: The Phantom Menace* he and fellow SF-based comedian Scott Capurro (Perrier Best Newcomer, 1994) played the pod race announcers. And from the sublime to the ridiculous, Proops is currently the voice of Bob the Builder in the American version of the eponymous animated kids show.

His main job, however, remains touring. He has made frequent visits to the Middle East to entertain American troops, where he steers clear of his more cynical political material and goes for the improvisation jugular. He has done weird corporate gigs, such as the one for IBM in Turkey where the audience turned up wearing togas. Last year he toured America again with Drew Carey doing an all-new improvisation show. Being on the road is vital to him: 'It's how I earn my living, but it is also how I generate new material. It's when I read newspapers – it's when things happen that I can put into my act.'

Wherever he plays, Proops always dresses and looks the same. He has an instantly identifiable image that you could almost turn into a cartoon character with a few brushstrokes. His name has become synonymous with the glasses, the quiff and the suit that is as smart as his banter. After all these years he is not about to get Trinny and Susannah in to do a makeover.

'I wouldn't change my look. Drew Carey had the eye operation so he doesn't have to wear glasses onstage, so he didn't for the first six months, then basically, he decided he had to go back. People weren't liking him so much, so now he wears a pair of spectacles with plain glass. When you are someone's TV friend you have to look like their TV friend when they see you. I don't mean to be a stickler but when I perform in a club I wear a suit and tie because that's what I wear on TV. You can't imagine how important it is. If I came on with long hair and a T-shirt you can't imagine the reaction. It's sort of a matter of keeping everybody with you. And also I'm obsessed with the look. It works for me. If you are trying to spend your whole life having a point of view and a persona, there is no point trying to break it into pieces bit by bit.'

And with that he downs his drink, gathers up his bag and heads over the Piccadilly Circus to meet up with the Comedy Store Players. It's thirty minutes to show-time but it doesn't matter. There is no need for a rehearsal – another joy of improvisation is there's no chance of forgetting your lines as you don't have any. After he is gone, however, I realize there's one question still unanswered.

Whatever did happen to Kelly Monteith?

Bruce Dessau

'Channel Tunnel'

Assembly Rooms, Edinburgh (1996),
Laughing Stock LAFFC 076

There are so many rules in this country …
Well, I guess it's not a surprise to you
guys. I think there are a lot of rules;
just slightly more rules than what, like,
oh Russia in the thirties? I couldn't bring
my cat over because all animals go into
quarantine — and thank you for your
sympathy by the way. [*Audience says, 'Aah'*]
Don't patronize me, I know the difference.

So I had to call like the feline bureau of,
like, pussy immigration or whatever it is.
And the guy throws a major huffy on me,
[*Puts on huffy voice*] 'No, no, no, we don't
let cats into the country, we just don't
let any animals into the country, all
animals that come in must be quarantined,
quarantined for six months, because this is
a non-rabies island; we don't have rabies.
There's no rabies on the island.' There's
also no, oh, healthcare or services on the
motorway … But rabies is very important,
because you know my cat is an imminent
rabies danger. My 18-year-old cat is going
to come over here and turn into Cujo? …

I thought it was unusual because people
love animals so much on this island. People
love animals here clearly more than they
love other people. You can die in a
hospital here, lay in the basement for

three days with no one finding you,
business as usual. Hey, stop whingeing.
What people really care about it is [*Puts
on voice*] 'I hope the veal calves haven't
had a bumpy ride to France, they haven't a
cushion to sit upon and the truck jostles
from side to side.' I can see being
concerned about a veal calf though; they're
fun … and delicious.

Now, I'm not saying you should be cruel to
animals, before you think I'm the most evil
piece of fuck that ever lived … You should
never be cruel to animals. It's not cool to
be cruel to animals … unless it's *funny*,
and then …

Okay, cats aren't supposed to fly, but when
they do … hee haw, hilarity ensues. You're
being very reserved and judgemental now,
but, if I did nothing all night but dip
cats into gasoline, stuff them in my ass,
light them on fire, shoot them across the
stage into a coffee tin while playing
'Whole Lot of Love' by Led Zeppelin, you
would never talk about anything else for
the rest of your lives … 'We saw Pavarotti
do Rigoletto.' 'Fuck that, I saw Greg
Proops shoot flaming cats out of his ass!
That's entertainment, that's comedy.' 'Did
he tell any jokes?' 'Jokes schmokes; he
shot flaming kitties. What do you want from
the man? He's working his heart out. James
Brown didn't shoot flaming cats out his ass
… The man is a genius'.

Now, that woman who got gored in Spain videotaping the bulls, I felt bad for her, but it proves my point about cows: when it comes to cattle, it's them or us, ladies and gentlemen. If a veal calf could eat you, it would. And it wouldn't care how comfortable a trip you had either. Hey, how was your ride? Moo … Crunch … That's it.

But somehow my cat is a hassle. My cat, my 18-year-old cat; my blind 18-year-old cat. [*Audience says, 'Ahh'*] Well see, now we're concerned. As soon as I give my cat a disability you're all on my side again. What if I told you I fed my cat flaming chunks of baby fucking veal? Then we wouldn't approve. Like my cat is going to lay into you at Heathrow. They're going to open the crate and the cat is going to pop out … 'Where are the British people? I want to bite them on the ass. I've got rabies … I'm blind, point me at them, where are they? Are those veal chunks I smell' ?

Now, am I wrong, or is there not a Chunnel that connects this island to Europe, right? Now, couldn't rats come through that Chunnel? Little saucy RABID French rats, with mischief on their minds? Couldn't they be coming through the Chunnel as we speak? [*Puts on huffy voice*] 'No, no, no, Greg, no rats are going to get through the Chunnel, we've thought of every contingency. No rats can come through because we built a screen, you see? And the screen will keep out the rats … Rubber stamp, rubber stamp; let's eat lunch.'

A screen; well hooby-goddam-doo. You know, rats aren't very good at survival. It's really a wonder they've made it this far, isn't it? And a lot of you are thinking, 'No Greg, they're pretty good at survival I think. You seem to be coming at this the wrong way. You see them everywhere; they do pretty well for themselves.' I KNOW … Certainly a screen will baffle and perplex them.

As we sit here, can little saucy French rats be coming through, right now, running through the Chunnel? [*Makes rat noises*] They get to the screen, and 'Oh! There's a screen; oh no, they're smarter than us. We're fucked. Allez. Attends. Allez, allez.' Now, you just know that there is some civil servant who has to stand at the end of that screen as the vast line of rabid French rats approaches, with like a cricket bat in his hand. [*Makes noise: 'Boom, crack'*] Sorted …

Speaking of teenagers, since we have so many in the house tonight, you remember that young man Peter Carey? I thought he was the most outstanding individual of this year. Remember when you were little and you'd get mad at your parents and you'd steal their passport and their credit cards and you'd fly all the way around the world? Remember when you'd do that? Wasn't childhood a kook fest? I don't remember having that much gumption. You know when you get mad at your parents you like go to the corner and just sulk pathetically. Not enough money for an ice cream; that's pathetic. And then crawl back home. [*Sobbing noise*] Hi mum. [*Bang*] Right in the head …

I don't remember stealing my dad's passport and credit cards and flying round the world to Singapore first class. That child could be president of my country. Nothing but respect for that kid.

And then they were going to put him on *The Word*. And I'm so sorry *The Word* went off the air. It's just typical, isn't it? All the good things in life. *The Word* was so good because, you know, there are TV programmers whose job it is to decide that Youth wants to watch a certain kind of show. As if Youth cares one way or the other what the fuck is on television. Don't you think Youth is a little busy on Friday night at 11.30? A little busy like taking ecstasy and shagging in cars and going to raves and stuff? You think what's on TV is really in their world?

You know who watched *The Word*? Fucking us: married over 30s losers, ladies and gentlemen, core audience for *The Word*, sitting there spellbound in front of the television. 'Oh my god! Look what those people are wearing. They're eating worms out of a bucket. Honey I can't move; go get me a beer, I can't move. Are we taping? Thank god we're taping. Wait till I show the kids when they get home .. '

I'll tell you about the United States a
little bit. Things are kind of freaky in
the United States right now. How do I
describe the state the country's in? Kind
of a Weimar Republic, Italy in the
thirties, I can't stand this rising-tide
kind of State. [*Audience applause*] Thank
you. Everything's taken this hideous turn
to the right, until it seems like the whole
country is being run by white, angry,
middle-aged male, psycho Christian, gun-
toting, truck-driving, neo-Nazi anti-choice
fuck-balls.

[*Cheering and clapping*]

Now, you may disagree; that's your
prerogative. I don't expect everyone to
agree; otherwise this would be like one bad
Star Trek episode or something …

Maybe you're an angry white male, although
what white men have to be angry about, I'm
not quite sure. Clearly everyone is
favoured ahead of us. I had to struggle
over so many Filipinos and Guyanese to get
my job. Struggle, I tell you! The problem
is this, the reason why America is such a
right-wing mess is clearly England's fault.
Thank you, that's been my show, and good
night …

I'll explain: because the Puritans, or as
we call them, the Pilgrims, came to America
274 years ago, and we still live by their
moral imperative. We're taught so many lies
in the United States. We celebrate
Thanksgiving, which I believe *here* is

called fuck-off Puritan day. And these are the lies they teach us in school. [*Puts on droning voice*]

The Pilgrims left England to escape religious persecution and to seek freedom in the New World. Mmmm ... bullshit! The Pilgrims were asked to leave this island. People couldn't wait to get the Pilgrims off this island. Plymouth was never more fun than when the Pilgrims left the island.

People were getting a little bit tired of right-wing psycho Christians walking around wearing all black with buckles *on their hats*, all carrying a musket, quoting the Bible to everyone: thou shalt not have fun, thou shalt not drink, all women are witches. Until people here went, 'Get the fuck off the island, sail across the ocean, go kill all the indigenous people in the New World, have a witch trial, let us know how that works out for you. We'll be hiding over here if anyone needs us. We'll be back in the mother land having a Renaissance if anyone needs us; you go over there, have some genocide, have some witch trials, let us know how that works out for you, okay'. [*Clapping*]

The post office here is so fantastic; it's the best value for money ... next to *Hello* magazine. There's all that entertainment, right? You stand in that queue, like, forever, watching the video with no sound on it, watching four women being dragged away and beaten up for not paying their TV

licences, then you get to the window and
there's all that glass, that huge Nazi war
criminal booth. If Kennedy had that much
glass he would still be alive today …

And the guy's behind the glass … 'I'd like
some stamps.' And he goes, 'What?' 'I'd
like some stamps.' 'What?' 'I'd like some
stamps.' 'What?' 'What the fuck else is
back there? What else can I buy? Give me
the washer dryer, the mink coat and the
Bentley; that's what I want. I know you got
it there; you've got a lot of special
merchandise back there.' 'What?' Ting,
ting, ting.

Then they give you the stamps, man; and
they always come through on that blackened
barbecue thing. Yes, that's right. And the
stamps are licking side down too! They
expect you to lick that stamp right after
it's come through on that blackened old
thing. And there's one sponge on the whole
island, it's in Aberdeen or somewhere.

It's only available at low tide across lava
rocks; you have to take your stamp. 'I'm
going to the sponge island honey, wish me
luck. Ow, there's sharks and puffins up my
ass. Moisten, moisten, moisten; I'm running
back now. I'd rather lick the ring road
clean than lick one of those stamps that
came through on that thing. It's like a
cracker that the cat dragged in.'

'English Pubs'

West Yorkshire Playhouse (1995),
Laughing Stock LAFFC 37

Like, say, you go to a poob. [*Laughter*] A
pub, a pub, okay?

And you want to drink, you want two drinks,
one for you, one for your matey. And I love
that, because if you called an American
matey, they'd go, are you a pirate? I like
your hook, matey, argh. Nice parrot, dude.

So, say you want a drink. You want two. You
want two gin and tonics, one for you, one
for your mate. Well, I learned immediately
that you don't go, TWO anything, because
you don't get that zesty positive response
… It seems to generate hostility. So I have
to go, well, 'I want one gin and tonic, and
then I want another. Two gin and tonics, is
how many I want. Get going, Nigel …'
[*Laughter*]

And the barman … oh-uh … oh, I've got to go
do my job. That's not in the job
description. Serving people? I'm a
playwright! So he takes a glass … and the
bottles aren't under the bar, because that
would be fun and easy and convenient.
[*Laughter*] The bottles are behind the bar
trapped against the wall, pinioned in
little puritan wooden bottle prisons,
because they've been very naughty bottles
indeed, haven't they, full of all that
lovely booze?

And they are upside down, being tortured,
so that they don't run away to Bottle Land.
[*Laughter*] There's a big party going on in
Bottle Land where the bottles are left to
roam freely to do what they will. They must
be imprisoned and held upside down.
[*Laughter*]

He takes a glass, sticks it under the
little dohickey that lets the booze out,
and out comes a measurement called a jill
or a gill or something? It's a Latin word
that means, no … No bloody booze whatsoever
is going to come out of this thing. A
scintilla. A jot. 'Did you put some gin in
there?' 'Yes.' 'You didn't put any gin in
there.' 'Give it to me. I'll drink it from
memory, okay?' 'I'll pretend I'm drunk …
And you pretend you're working'.

Now, he takes the glass and… and they don't
have a bar gun to put the tonic in …
They've got those little bottles, those
little dinky bottles. They produce one like
a magician's assistant. Out it comes, a
little bottle. They're just darling. They …
they're just … they're little Hummel
figures. They're cute. Collect them. Trade
them. Get the whole set. [*Laughter*] But to
the mayor of Dinky Town, to Papa Smurf,
[*Laughter*] the bottles are huge. Bilbo the
Hobbit would go, 'My god, that bottle's
enormous.' But to humans the bottle's this
bloody big. So he pours it in. Now there's
nothing in the glass. In essence, it's a
memory of booze and a jot of tonic.

So now the hard part … 'excuse me, could I … could I … could I bother you? Could I get … please, could I get some ice in my … in my drink' ?

It's a huge wall of resentment that I must hurdle. [*Laughter*] He goes over to a Watney's bucket that's been sitting there since, like, 1584. It's never been cleaned. You don't know what's going on inside this Watney's bucket. He opens up the lid.

It's like Jurassic Park. There's raptors in there. He takes out a really long spoon, a really long, long spoon with a lot of curves in it, because you don't want to get too close to ice … [*Laughter*]

Because obviously anyone who orders ice is a witch and must be kept away with the huge spoon of salvation. 'Get away, witch. You want ice. You're not from our land'.

He takes it. He's going to put it in the glass. They're not cubes. Oh no. They're those little round things, but they've melted and they're sad and pathetic and now they've formed a little crescent, a little Islamic Jihad terrorist cube … [*Laughter*] that can wedge up under your soft palate. And they don't clink when they hit the bottom of the glass. They don't clink when they hit because they're so sad. There's nothing left of them. They don't clink together because … [*Laughter*] 'I'm melting … help me, I'm melting…'

Now, again, America's not better because we have ice. We have drive-by shootings in the United States, which you guys don't have. And, frankly, you're big fat pussies, but the point is, if you're shot in a drive-by shooting in the United States an ambulance will speed to the scene. A paramedic leaps out and he puts a big bag of ice right on your bullet wound. That's service, ladies and gentlemen.

12. MONTY PYTHON'S FLYING CIRCUS

Pining for the fjords ...

It could have been 'Toad Elevating Moment'. It might have been 'Owl-Stretching Time'. For a brief moment it was 'El Turbot's Flying Circus'. And 'Vaseline Review'. And 'Ow! It's Colin Plint' and then 'Ow, It's Arthur Megapode's Flying Circus' and then 'Brian Stalin's Flying Circus'. It probably would have been 'Bunn, Wackett, Buzzard, Stubble and Boot', but someone high up at the BBC thought that was silly.

At one point it was 'Gwen Dibley's Flying Circus'. Michael Palin had seen the name in a Women's Institute magazine at his mother-in-law's house and rather liked the idea of this stranger opening the *Radio Times* and seeing that there was a programme named after her. Guilt took over, however, plus the fact that he thought there might be copyright issues. Palin might have been onto something though. Someone somewhere is surely writing a PhD on the use of the name 'Dibley' in British comedy. Apart from its brief cameo here, it famously became the name of the village in which Dawn French was the vicar. And Duane Dibley was the anorak-wearing alter ego of *Red Dwarf*'s Cat. But for now the name was consigned to history.

And so, at 11 pm on 5 October 1969, the recently christened not-silly-at-all *Monty Python's Flying Circus* aired for the first time. It was a show that would revolutionize television comedy, taking it out of the black-and-white past and into the dazzling multihued future. It wasn't the first example of surreal, colourful comedy that dispensed with punchlines – Spike Milligan's *Q5* had been launched earlier in the year – but Python was a showcase for the next generation of comedy talents that had been waiting to explode into the mainstream.

Most of the participants had been knocking on the doors of television fame since the tail-end of the early sixties satire boom, and by the latter half of the decade decided to pool their resources. Michael Palin and Terry Jones had worked their way via the *Oxford Revue* to cult children's show *Do Not Adjust your Set* (curious fact: this also featured a very young David Jason), when they teamed up with Cambridge Footlights alumni Eric Idle and John Cleese and Graham Chapman. The latter duo had formed a successful writing partnership who had worked on *At Last the 1948 Show* (*see* Chapter 1). Their career paths had all already overlapped and re-crossed on the successor to *That Was the Week that Was*, *The Frost Report*, fronted by David Frost.

Completing the team was American animator extraordinary Terry Gilliam. And the comedy matchmaker who brought them to the BBC was consultant/producer Barry Took. Did I mention that the show was also provisionally titled 'Baron von Took's Flying Circus'?

The first series didn't get huge audience figures – regional opt-outs and breaks in the run to transmit sporting events made sure of that. But three million viewers for a graveyard slot was not bad at all, and it garnered those all-important critical plaudits assuring a second series.

There are plenty of classic moments in the first of their four BBC runs. Eric Idle going, 'Nudge, nudge'; 'Hell's Grannies', featuring a bunch of marauding, delinquent geriatrics; 'The Lumberjack Song', about a wannabe cross-dressing mighty Redwood-chopper; and, of course, the man with a tape recorder up his nose and the man with a tape recorder up his brother's nose. All this, and Terry Gilliam's dizzyingly nightmarish animations too.

And then, in Episode 8 there was 'The Parrot Sketch', featured here. The plot is fiendishly simple. John Cleese plays Mr Praline, a disgruntled customer, all plastered down hair and plastic raincoat, who goes into a pet shop to complain about a bird he bought there that is no longer breathing. Michael Palin plays the shopkeeper who is polite but reluctant to acknowledge there is a problem. 'He's just resting,' he suggests. 'Beautiful plumage,' he explains.

And so the dispute escalates, with Cleese eventually throwing the dead parrot to the floor in despair. In the original television version, Palin suggests he tries taking it to his brother's shop in Ipswich. Cleese goes out, returns to the same shop except that Palin is now wearing a moustache. Cleese goes puce with rage, but the matter remains unresolved until Graham Chapman's Colonel arrives to suggest that they should end things now because they are getting silly.

In the original episode, the audience response is relatively restrained. Yet over the years 'The Parrot Sketch' has attained almost mystical status as a definitive piece of Python. In November 2004, in a *Radio Times* poll, it was voted the Greatest Comedy Sketch of all time, knocking *Little Britain*'s Lou and Andy into second spot. Five months later, in a Channel 4 poll of the 50 Greatest Comedy Sketches of all time the first and second positions were reversed, but I would hazard a guess that, in a decade, the dead parrot will still feature in the Top Ten, while *Little Britain*'s creations may have slipped significantly out of favour.

One of the reasons for its popularity may be that unlike some other memorable Python moments it does not push the comedy envelope particularly far. The dispute can be appreciated by all generations as a simple variation on the 'two-men-and-a-desk' format. This traditional format would continue with the *Two Ronnies*' Four Candles/Fork Handles classic, which has also featured regularly in the upper echelons of various comedy charts. Cleese naturally adds a class element to the dialogue which the British viewer is hard-wired to love. In fact, listening to it again reveals that Cleese is not even playing Mr Praline as one of his off-the-peg chinless authoritarian toffs, but the master/servant dynamic lends the sketch that inevitable undertow.

Further humour comes from the contrast between Cleese's increasingly exasperated ranting and the unflappable Palin. It cleverly subverts the very British received notion of the customer being right. Here the customer is patently correct and yet the man on the other side of the counter refuses to acknowledge the truth that is staring him in the face: 'This parrot wouldn't "voom" if you put 4 million volts through it.'

Python, for all its radicalism, used the two-hander format on a regular basis. There was the 'Argument' sketch, in which people go to a room and pay to have an argument with a man behind a desk. Elsewhere, Eric Idle played numerous annoying customers, including a man who talked constantly in verse. The simple secret was subverting expectations – who pays for an argument? What does a cheese shop not have in stock? Straightforward twists of logic, exquisitely executed.

Like 'The Four Yorkshiremen' sketch featured here (for discussion, *see* Chapter 1), 'The Parrot Sketch' has its origins in the pre-Python years. In 1968 John Cleese was having a chat with his occasional performing partner Michael Palin, who was telling him about his local garage, where, whenever you took back a car with a problem the mechanic would deny there was a problem. In the *Pythons Autobiography by the Pythons* (Orion) Cleese shed further light on the story: 'The guy would say, "Lovely car, lovely car," and Mike would say, "Well, yes, but I'm having trouble with the clutch ...." "Sticky clutch in the first 2000 miles? it's the sign of good quality."' Cleese and his regular writing partner Graham Chapman thought there was something in this, and wrote it up as a sketch featuring Chapman as the customer and Palin as an oily car salesman for a one-off BBC show entitled *How to Irritate People*.

Eighteen months later, the Python ensemble was kicking about ideas, and the talk turned to this sketch. Cleese recalled how he thought it had more mileage: 'I thought it had got something funny in it, but the car was too hackneyed.' For a while there was talk of a new version about returning a faulty toaster, before the idea of relocating it to a pet shop came up. After a bit of debate between Cleese and Chapman as to whether it should concern the return of a dog or a parrot, the parrot won.

Soon after transmission, the sketch began to gather momentum. In some eyes, it was even being interpreted as having political significance. Later, in 1989 at the Aspen Comedy Festival, Cleese revealed that two weeks after it first went out someone had come up to him and said: 'It's about the Vietnam war, isn't it.'

When it was featured in the 1972 Python movie, *And Now for Something Completely Different,* it gained a further push up the comedy rankings. This film – essentially previously seen clips re-shot for the big screen in a disused milk depot in north London – was no artistic breakthrough, but it was a sign of celluloid things to come. The only real change was that Palin confessed he had never wanted to be a shopkeeper anyway, allowing him to walk into a different set and break into 'The Lumberjack Song'.

The musical number seemed to become the established way to finish the sketch. It was done like this when the Pythons appeared at the Drury Lane Theatre in February 1973. These live shows came as a shock to the team and made them realize the true impact of the show. On television, they did their material and the polite studio audiences laughed in all the right places. On stage, however, there would be an outburst of hysteria as soon as it was apparent which sketch was being performed. The simple opening line, 'I wish to register a complaint,' was enough to bring the house down. It was as if this was a pop group on stage, and their greatest hits were being cheered when the first chord was struck. It sometimes made performances hard. Try to pause for comic effect, and there was a huge risk that someone in the audience would shout out your next line for you. 'Ours was the only show where you could get a prompt from the audience,' said Eric Idle at Aspen.

Cleese and Palin had a similar experience again during their April 1976 appearance at the first Amnesty International gala at Her Majesty's Theatre, Haymarket, known as 'A Poke in the Eye (With a Sharp Stick)'. This is the version featured here, regarded by many to be the best-ever rendition. By this time, the sketch has already taken on iconic status for a number of reasons. After four series, Python had called it a day television-wise, and John Cleese had left after three series anyway to pursue other ventures including *Fawlty Towers* (though if he wanted to live the sketch down why did he call Basil Fawlty's long-suffering maid Polly?), so there was considerable excitement seeing him revisiting past glories.

By this time, the series had also been discovered by the nascent American cable network and the group was well on their way to becoming megastars on the other side of the Atlantic. But this was no celebratory revival or lap of honour. The reason Cleese and Palin chose to do it was that they needed something they knew backwards, as there was little time for rehearsal. There was also no room for a big set: the only props were a cage, a stuffed bird, a table and a brown overcoat for Palin.

In recent years, Cleese has confessed that he was bored by the sketch as well as other bits of work: 'I get fed up with it. Repetition kills everything.' Even back then, he chose to spice things up a little to amuse himself and keep it interesting. This is partly what makes this version so funny. Cleese plays around with the format, by adding extra emphasis, extra drama and most of all, ad libbing to make Michael Palin corpse and remarking, 'This is nothing to laugh at,' when he does.

Looking back at the footage for a BBC *Arena* documentary 25 years later, Palin saw it afresh and enjoyed the sight of Cleese thwacking the parrot on the tabletop. 'I've never seen John at such high voltage. If there was an Olympic sport of parrot bashing he'd win it hands down.' But the audience did nearly put a spanner in the works. They were laughing because they knew what was coming and that threw the duo's timing off. Palin's awareness of what was imminent took its toll too. He was on the verge of breaking into hysterics as Cleese waited as long as possible before exploding into the, 'Pining for the fjords,' pay-off.

This appearance cemented the sketch's place in comedy legend. Even successive generations who publicly proclaimed a deep-seated mistrust of the Python brigade, and had got into comedy as a reaction against them, secretly harboured a love of it. The Comedy Store scene was supposed to be anti-Oxbridge and a reaction to Python, yet Rik Mayall told writer Roger Wilmut: 'We had a down on the Pythons. Although we all secretly thought that the Pythons were great, and half of us were redbrick and university anyway.'

The nineties generation of comedians also venerated the Pythons. Vic Reeves told me how, when he used to watch it, he laughed so much he fell off the sofa and was sick. Along with Spike Milligan and *Top of the Pops*, it was one of the few television spots he made a point of watching. 'I never watched telly anyway. I used to spend most of my time listening to the radio, climbing trees and pretending I was a space alien.' The influence was certainly clear in Reeves and Mortimer's total disregard for anything resembling a conventional punchline or linear narrative.

The sketch did not just linger in the back of every fan's mind – even the Pythons themselves couldn't quite leave it alone. They did it together again for Amnesty International in 1989 at 'The Secret Policeman's Biggest Ball'. And they had an all-new ending this time to make it topical. Palin happily concurred with Cleese's diagnosis that the bird was a stiff and offered him a couple of holiday vouchers as compensation. Cleese paused for a moment then replied: 'Well, you can't say Thatcher hasn't changed some things.'

Ironically, Margaret Thatcher herself had a bash at reworking the lines to write off the Liberal Democrats at the Conservative's 1990 Conference. In the process, she revealed that there is a lot more to comedy than getting the right words in the right order. Palin recalled that the Pythons considered suing for breach of copyright. They might have had a stronger case for prosecuting her performance as a crime against humour.

And so, despite being murdered by one ex-prime minister and nearly disowned by one of its creators, the dead parrot lives on. Popular culture continues to pay homage in numerous ways. In *Buffy the Vampire Slayer,* a victorious battle with an Egyptian villain closed with the lines, 'This mummy hand has ceased to be. It is an ex-mummy's hand.' A special *South Park* tribute featured Cartman and Kyle reworking it to mark the umpteenth killing of Kenny.

Following the death of Graham Chapman in 1989, what could have been a more fitting tribute at his memorial service than the one delivered by John Cleese. 'Graham Chapman is no more, he has gone to meet his maker, he has rung down the curtain and joined the choir invisible.'

As for Python themselves, they live on in cyberspace and on DVD, where a whole new generation is discovering them. *Little Britain*'s Matt Lucas is a fan and wasn't even born when the first series was transmitted. Meanwhile, *Spamalot*, the musical version of *Monty Python and the Holy Grail*, has been a hit on Broadway, and at the time of writing is due to open in London's fashionable West End in October 2006. You may even be able to buy Ben and Jerry's latest flavour of ice cream, 'Vermonty Python', in the interval.

And, as for John Cleese, the man who was bored with repeating himself three decades ago? He recently performed in a solo show in New Zealand. Did he do 'The Parrot Sketch'? Of course he didn't. Well, not exactly. But he did reportedly do a dead sheep sketch ...

Bruce Dessau

'The Parrot Sketch'

'A Poke in the Eye (With a Sharp Stick)' (Amnesty gala),
Her Majesty's Theatre, London (1976),
Laughing Stock LAFFCD 107

CLEESE

I wish to register a complaint. [*Laughter, applause*] [*Clearing throat*]

Hello, Miss.

PALIN

What do you mean, Miss?

CLEESE

I'm sorry. I have a cold.

[*Laughter*]

I wish to make a complaint.

PALIN

Sorry, we're closed for lunch.

CLEESE

Never mind that, my lad. I wish to complain about this parrot that I purchased not half an hour ago from this very boutique.

PALIN

Oh yes, the … the Norwegian Blue. What's … what's wrong with it?

CLEESE

I'll tell you what's wrong with it, my lad. It's dead. That's what's wrong with it.

[*Laughter*]

PALIN

No, no, it … it's resting.

[*Laughter*]

CLEESE

Look, matey, I know a dead parrot when I see one and I'm looking at one right now.

[*Laughter*]

PALIN

No, no, he's … he's not dead, squire. He's resting. Remarkable bird, the Norwegian Blue, isn't it, hey? *Beautiful* plumage.

[*Laughter*]

CLEESE

The plumage don't enter into it. He's stone dead.

PALIN

No, no, he's resting.

CLEESE

All right then. If he's resting, I'll wake him up. Hello, Polly parrot. I've got a lovely delicious fresh cuttlefish for you if you …

PALIN

  There, he moved!

CLEESE

  No, he didn't. That was you hitting the
  cage.

  [*Laughter*]

PALIN

  I never.

CLEESE

  Yes, you did.

PALIN

  I didn't.

CLEESE

  Hello, Polly. [*Laughter*] Wakey-wakey.
  [*Knocking*] Testing… [*Knocking*] Show a leg.
  [*Knocking*] [*Laughter*] This is your nine o'
  clock alarm call. [*Knocking*] [*Laughter*,
  applause] Now, that's what I call a dead
  parrot.

PALIN

  No, no, he's stunned.

  [*Laughter*]

CLEESE

  Stunned?

PALIN

Yes. You stunned him just as he was waking up. Norwegian Blues stun easily.

[*Laughter*]

CLEESE

Now listen matey, I've had enough of this. That parrot is definitely deceased and when I purchased it not half an hour ago, you assured me that its total lack of movement was due to it being tired and shagged out after a prolonged squawk.

PALIN

Well, he's … he's probably pining for the fjords.

[*Laughter*]

CLEESE

Pining for the fjords? [*Laughter, applause*] Pining for the fjords? [*Voice rising hysterically*] What kind of talk is that? [*Laughter*] Look, this is nothing to laugh at. Why did he fall … [*Laughter*] Why did he fall flat on his back the moment I got him home?

PALIN

The Norwegian Blue prefers kipping on his back. A remarkable bird, eh squire? Beautiful plumage.

[*Laughter*]

CLEESE

Look, I took the liberty of examining that bird when I got it home and I discovered that the only reason it had been sitting on its perch in the first place, was that it had been nailed there.

[*Laughter*]

PALIN

Well, of course it was nailed there. If I hadn't nailed that bird down it would've muscled up to them bars, bent them apart with its beak and … 'voom'.

CLEESE

'Voom'? Mate, this parrot wouldn't 'voom' if you put four million volts through it. [*Laughter*] It's bleeding demised.

PALIN

No, no. He's pining.

CLEESE

He's not pining. He's passed on. This parrot is no more. [*Laughter*] He has ceased to be. It's a stiff, bereft of life. He rests in peace. He's snuffed it. He's hopped the twig and kicked the bucket. He's shuffled off this mortal coil, run down the curtains and joined the bleeding choir invisible. He's extinct in his entirety. This is an ex-parrot. [*Laughter, applause*]

PALIN

Well, I better replace it then.

CLEESE

If you want to get anything done in this country, you've got to go … [*Laughter*]

PALIN

Sorry, squire, I've had a look around the back and we're right out of parrots.

CLEESE

I see. I see. I get the picture.

PALIN

I've got a slug?

[*Laughter*]

CLEESE

Does it talk?

PALIN

Not really.

CLEESE

Well, it's scarcely a replacement, is it? [*Knocking sound*] Bleeding slug.

PALIN

Listen, mate, I didn't want to be a pet shop owner anyway. You know what I wanted to be? I wanted to be a lumberjack. [*Applause, cheering*] Leaping from tree to tree as they float down the mighty rivers of British Columbia. [*Cheering*]

CLEESE

I tell you, you can't get service anywhere
nowadays.

PALIN

The giant redwood, the larch, the fir, the
mighty Scot's pine, the smell of fresh cut
timber, the crash of mighty trees …

[*Laughter, applause*]

'The Four Yorkshiremen'

'The Secret Policeman's Ball' (Amnesty gala),
Her Majesty's Theatre, London (1979),
Laughing Stock LAFFCD 107

[*Music, footsteps, applause*]

JONES

Very passable indeed, eh?

ALL

Aye.

ATKINSON

You can't beat a good glass of Chateau de Chasselas, eh, Josiah?

JONES

You're right there, Obediah.

CLEESE

Who'd have thought 40 year ago we'd be sitting here drinking Chateau de Chasselas?

ALL

Aye

JONES

In them days we were glad to have the price of a cup of tea.

ATKINSON

Aye. A cup of cold tea.

ALL

  Aye.

CLEESE

  Without milk …

PALIN

  or sugar …

ATKINSON

  Or tea.

  [*Laughter*]

PALIN

  Aye. In a cracked cup and all.

CLEESE

  We never had a cup. We used to drink out of
  a rolled up newspaper.

  [*Laughter*]

ATKINSON

  Best we could do was to suck on a piece of
  damp cloth.

JONES

  But, you know, we were happy in those days,
  though we were poor.

PALIN

  Because we were poor. My old dad used to
  say to me, money doesn't buy you happiness,
  son.

CLEESE

And he was right.

JONES

Right, he were.

CLEESE

I was happier then. We had nothing. We used
to live in a tiny old tumbledown house with
great holes in roof.

ATKINSON

A house?

[*Laughter*]

You were lucky to have a house. We used to
live in one room, 26 of us, no furniture
and half the floor was missing. [*Laughter*]
Huddled in one corner for fear of falling.

JONES

Well, you were lucky to have a room. We
used to have to live in corridor.

PALIN

Oh, we used to dream of living in a
corridor.

[*Laughter, applause*]

PALIN

It would've been a palace to us. We used to
live in an old water tank at a rubbish tip.
[*Laughter*] Got woken up every morning by
having a load of rotting fish dumped all
over us. House? Hah.

CLEESE

Well, when I say house, it were only a hole
in the ground covered by a couple of foot
of torn canvas, but it were house to us.

[*Laughter*]

ATKINSON

We were evicted from our hole in the
ground. [*Laughter*] We had to go live in
lake.

[*Laughter*]

JONES

You were lucky to have a lake. There were
150 of us living in shoebox in middle of
motorway.

PALIN

Cardboard box?

JONES

Aye.

PALIN

You were lucky.

[*Laughter*]

We lived for three months in a rolled up
newspaper in a septic tank. [*Laughter*] We
used to have to get up at six every
morning, clean the newspaper, eat a crust
of stale bread, go to work down mill, 14
hours a day, week in, week out for sixpence

a month and when we got home, our dad would thrash us to sleep with belt.

[*Laughter*]

ATKINSON

Luxury.

[*Laughter*]

We used to have to get out of the lake at 3 am, clean the lake, eat a handful of hot gravel, work 20 hours a day at the mill for tuppence a month, come home, and dad would beat us about the head and neck with a broken bottle, if we were lucky.

[*Laughter*]

JONES

Well, of course, we had it tough. [*Laughter*] We used to have to get up out of shoebox in middle of night and lick the road clean with our tongues. [*Laughter*] We had half handful of cold gravel, worked 24 hours a day at mill for four pence every six years and when we got home our dad would slice us in two with bread knife.

[*Laughter*]

CLEESE

Right.

I used to get up in the morning at half past ten at night half an hour before I went to bed … [*Laughter, applause*] eat a lump of freezing cold poison, work 28 hours a day at mill and pay mill owner to let us work there and when I got home, our dad used to murder us in cold blood each night and dance about on our graves singing 'Hallelujah' …

[*Laughter, applause*]

PALIN

Now, you try and tell the young people of today that and they won't believe you.

ALL

No … they won't believe you …

[*Laughter, applause, cheering*]

13. MARK THOMAS

Playing the system

Mark Thomas has always been a bit of a troublemaker. When he was a scholarship boy at the exclusive Christ's Hospital School in Surrey, punk happened. Pupils were forbidden from having spiky hair. Maybe the teachers thought it clashed with the traditional gowns everyone had to wear at all times. Thomas had his own solution. He went further, to a place beyond the rules. He had a skinhead haircut.

Thomas describes his default behaviour setting as 'cussedness'. This has stood him in good stead in his stand-up comedy career, which started back in 1985 when he played Putney's Fat Cat Club and was, by his own admission, 'shit'. He was not shit for long. Otherwise, his wisecracking, fast-talking political patter, inspired by everyone from the Clash to Bertolt Brecht, has never really changed: 'Sometimes there have been knob gags, sometimes there has been pure filth, but there has always been politics. Green issues, smut, vaguely tinged with social conscience in the early days. I remember doing a sub-Keith Allen routine about cops being beaten up with alabaster soap dishes in Knightsbridge. I've always been playing the system.'

His sense of justice might well be something that runs in the Thomas family. Turning off his iPod and catching his breath, in a light, airy central London boardroom on a stormy May afternoon, he rattles through his biographical essentials: 'I was born on 11th April, 1963. My mum was a midwife and my dad was a self-employed builder. He was also a lay preacher, which is probably more significant than I would wish. My great granddad was a Baptist nonconformist preacher; my sister is a vicar. She always jokes that I narrowly avoided the family business.'

He spent much of his childhood hanging around various churches in the Clapham area, but in his teens Thomas lost his faith. By the time he got to Christ's Hospital (curious fact: Barnes Wallis, the inventor of the Bouncing Bomb, was also educated here – perhaps Thomas's gags are like verbal bouncing bombs, building up slowly until they hit their final target in an explosive punchline), the subversive Thomas philosophy fans know today was fully formed: 'Me and my mates did the most horrible things in churches. They used to have these boxes for sheet music and we'd go and urinate in them and put them back on the shelves. I do think I'm often conflicted about whether to get on and enjoy life or take part in the struggle, and that maybe sums me up.'

Summing up what Thomas does for a living in a couple of words is a little harder. 'Am I a stand-up comedian or a satirist? I've given up. My thing is you can either go, "It's very funny theatre," or you can say, "It's political stand-up that's less funny than your Comedy Store intense gag factory." You can look at it from either end of the spectrum.' He pauses and purses his lips. 'Besides, as I've got older I don't give a fuck any more what people think of me.' He certainly has fans in high places. *The Guardian* called him 'John Pilger with laughs,' while there can't be many Perrier Award nominees who have had a column in the thinking left-winger's magazine the *New Statesman*.

At Christ's Hospital,, Thomas balanced his love of the Clash with his love of political theatre: 'I saw Brecht's Caucasian Chalk Circle when I was 16 and I was amazed that my mind was changed by something on stage. I thought one thing when I walked in and another when I walked out.' He hadn't really considered a career in comedy yet – 'comedians never make business plans' – but he did become aware of the power of words and was intrigued by the way an idea could be conveyed in front of an audience.

After school, Thomas went to Bretton Hall in Yorkshire to study drama. 'The interesting thing about it was that my dad was really proud because I was the first member of the family to go to college, but he was slightly dubious because it was a drama college. When I went home and told him about wearing tights in the dance and movement class, his shocked response was like something out of a kitchen sink drama. But for the first time ever I was with a group of people who had similar ideas. It was 1984, around the time of the miners' strike. We used to write plays, do gigs at soup kitchens, on picket lines. You'd write the show, then perform it the next day. Half were shit, but half were a real laugh, and that's where it all gelled. It was like sketches and songs, really surreal and odd.'

Thomas was away at college when the alternative comedy scene became established in London. But, going home in the holidays, he quickly caught up and thought about trying it himself. 'I used to go to the original branch of Jongleurs which me and my dad had decorated when it was a roller disco in the late seventies.' Thomas saw the early pioneers of political humour – Tony Allen, Bob Boyton, Claire Dowie – on the burgeoning London circuit. 'Then a friend played me Alexei Sayle's album and it was like a bolt from the blue, an amazing thing. He was my hero and still is. John Cleese said of Peter Cook that he was the gatekeeper of modern comedy. Sayle wasn't the gatekeeper, he just kicked the gate down.'

Thomas was determined to become a part of the vibrant comedy scene. After college, when he was working on a building site, at lunchtimes he would go to the local newsagent and pick up a copy of *Time Out*. Then, in a phone box, he would go through the entire comedy section ringing venues one by one, until someone offered him a spot. He was always short of time, anxiously wolfing down his sandwiches while waiting for a return call.

After his spectacularly bad debut in November 1985, Thomas quickly started to improve. The challenge was finding the right balance between the political agenda and the punchlines. Thomas realized that there was no point standing on stage saying what he believed, or being provocative, if it wasn't funny. It was the humour that got the message across and made his audience think. Over the next few months, he learnt the art of working a room and how to craft a stand-up set.

But even the best comedians have some awful gigs where they die a thousand deaths. Back in the eighties, there weren't so many places to play, so you took your chances whenever you had a booking. One night, Thomas was booked to appear at the Oxford Polytechnic Graduation Ball. No-one was there to see the comedy: they just wanted to drink as much alcohol as they could and then, if still capable, have a meaningless sexual encounter. The previous act had been heckled for two solid minutes, sprayed with champagne, and then carried off stage, leaving Thomas to hold the fort. Through no fault of his own, Thomas was asked to leave the stage after five minutes, and had to make his miserable way back to London.

Gigging outside London was rarely a luxurious affair. After the show, it was a choice of grim digs or the long journey home. After a show in Glasgow, Thomas was invited to stay at a student house. The sheets were so filthy, covered in dubious stains, that he slept fully clothed. Sometimes un-sophisticated audiences wanted the kind of crude politically incorrect gags that Roy 'Chubby' Brown could deliver in his sleep, but Thomas couldn't deliver if there was a gun pointed at his head. When someone shouted out, 'Tell us a period joke,' Thomas's rapid-fire response was, 'Two Elizabethans walk into a pub ...'

Apart from Alexei Sayle, there was another influence on Thomas who is less obvious but who also fed directly into the development of his style. 'Dave Allen was a genius. He told brilliant stories, was as funny as fuck and was always an outsider. He was required viewing in my family. Dave Allen was really the start, then I used to love the Goons. When I was at boarding school, my mates and I were really homesick and a mate's uncle used to send us Goon Show tapes. When I was 12, I directed and starred in a Goon Show play at school.'

Woody Allen is another unlikely influence, as is Les Dawson. 'He was as important to me as the Clash or plays by Bertolt Brecht.' While growing up Thomas was unaware of the legendary angry American satirist that he often gets compared to: 'I didn't even know who Lenny Bruce was until I started working on the circuit. Then I got his books out and they were shit. A few good lines but shit. But he was dead and he took drugs, which made him a rock and roll comic.'

If politics was the priority at the outset, after a while the gag became paramount for Thomas. Now that he has become adept at both making people laugh and saying something important, he is not so sure whether politics or comedy comes first. It is probably a dead heat: 'It's all one big lump and the rest of the world seems out of step.' Channel 4 has clearly found Thomas equally uncategorizable. Over the years, his provocative, playful programmes have been made by both the comedy team and the current affairs department.

His early stunts and imaginative pranks on *The Mark Thomas Comedy Product* have gone down in comedy history. He drove a tank decked out as an ice cream van to Tory cabinet minister William Waldegrave's office. He organized a mass paging of MPs at the Labour Party Conference, so that when Jack Straw finished a speech they spontaneously broke out in a robotic chorus of 'Encore'. And he got so many viewers to ask to see ex-Tory armed forces minister Nicholas Soames's antique furniture – as they were entitled to under a tax exemption scheme – that Soames stumped up the tax to protect his privacy and his palatial home from the plebs.

Then there was the time when Thomas went to Sellafield and proved that local seagull shit was radioactive. And the time he tried to break sanctions by exporting a teddy bear to Iraq. Despite Thomas's opinion that comedy on its own cannot change much, he did have an effect. A loophole in Inheritance Tax rules was closed by Gordon Brown after Thomas stuck his oar in, and Nestlé changed the labelling for baby milk in certain African countries after he became involved.

Over the years his programme mutated, becoming more than just a send-up of the gullible, the great and the good. Eventually even the title changed, to *The Mark Thomas Product*. But comedy was still at the heart of everything Thomas did. He was able to unearth the funny side, even when dealing with arms manufacturers and traders, who shamelessly tried to sell him their deadly products as if they were as harmless as washing machines. His probes into the Labour government's behaviour clearly made their mark. The minister for trade at the time, Richard Caborn, allegedly asked civil servants to dig for dirt on Thomas.

His only regret is the one that got away. 'I tried hard to get Jeffrey Archer. I remember driving past his big flat which overlooks the Thames, and it has this enormous great plastic poppy on the balcony, so I phoned up Lambeth Council and said I want to report an unsafe structure.' It is interesting to note that, when Thomas started doing these political pranks, he was completely unaware that Michael Moore was doing a similar thing in America. He has learnt to live with the comparison these days, smiling politely when Moore's name comes up, as it frequently does. Thomas admires a lot of Moore's work. They've met, and have even done fundraising gigs together.

But whereas Moore comes from a counter-cultural journalistic background, Thomas's roots are firmly in the comedy camp. He has very cannily managed to balance his television output with his live work, and he still tours whenever he can. One memorable live show explored the links between Coca-Cola and Germany in the 1930s, and explained how Fanta was invented because German factories couldn't get the ingredients to make Coke. He invited audience members to suggest possible ad campaigns that the Nazis might have come up with to sell the drinks, and subsequently held a touring exhibition. After a period when political comedy fell out of favour, it is undoubtedly back in vogue. Thomas's 2006 double header tour with Robert Newman played to packed houses throughout the country.

'Comedy is almost like a movement in its own right,' says Thomas, as he warms to his theme. 'Robert Wyatt, one of my heroes, described himself as a cheerleader for change, and maybe that's what comedians do. Just look at the way John Prescott's authority has been eroded by all the jokes about him doing the rounds.' Comedy's strength is its ability to spread the word through unofficial channels. That's what makes gigging so special. In an age when you can find almost any opinion being expressed on Google, actually seeing someone in the flesh express what you are thinking has a greater impact than ever. And if they can make you laugh at the same time, the message is even more likely to get through.

One of Thomas's most recent outings on the small screen was a *Dispatches* special, in which he exposed dubious practices in the arms trade by getting schoolchildren to set themselves up as arms dealers to show how easy it was. 'Lovely kids,' he grins. The global trade in weapons and instruments of torture is Thomas's enduring fixation. He is so obsessed by it he has even corrected civil servants by quoting obscure documents at them. A few years ago he was charged with criminal damage after attaching himself by a bicycle lock to a bus full of arms dealers near Tower Bridge, who were on their way to a trade fair in Docklands. He was acquitted and got some great comic material out of it. He has recorded some of his experiences in his book, *As Used on the Famous Nelson Mandela* (Ebury). The title, by the way, comes from an advert for leg-irons.

Thomas is a passionate advocate of the power of satire, but believes it can only really be a part of major change, and, despite his own achievements, can rarely prompt change in its own right. 'It has to be a part of a bigger political campaign.' However, he does take great pride in the fact that, two thirds of the way through the tour of his show based around the fight to stop the Ilisu dam being built in Turkey, the finance for the deal collapsed. 'The deal just fell on its face. The campaign caused that, but the Dambusters show was about the campaign and played its part in it.' An excerpt from that routine featuring Thomas on fiery form is included here.

'The deal was to build a dam which would displace about 78,000 Kurds in the Kurdish region of Turkey. Human rights abuses against the Kurds are shocking,' he explains. 'There were people in prison for signing petitions saying they want to be taught in the Kurdish language, whole villages were destroyed. The building of the dam meant a scorched earth policy in the region. We started the campaign, bum-rushed the shareholders' meetings, used every trick that we could, and after three years the project collapsed.'

His efforts did not go unnoticed. In 2002, Thomas was presented with the Kurdish National Congress Medal of Honour and a Human Rights Award from the Kurdish Human Rights Project. Not bad for someone who used to piss in the chapel sheet music boxes at school.

Bruce Dessau

'Christians and Drugs'

Birmingham Rep Theatre (1995),
Laughing Stock LAFFCD 78

[*Applause*]

If you are sitting out there, per chance, and you are a Christian, and you will know whether you're a Christian because you'll be beginning to air tambourine 'Kum Ba Yah, My Lord' by now …

[*Laughter*]

I often wonder whether Salvation Army kids air tambourine in the bedroom?

[*Laughter*].

But anyway, if you are Christian and you are sitting out there, you will know that you are a Christian because you will be feeling a little bit picked upon and a little bit victimized at this point, but fuck it, if it's good enough for Jesus … [*Applause*].

'It's not fair, we went to this thing and Mark picked on me for being a Christian.'

'Did he put nails through your hands?'

'No.'

'Well stop fucking whining …'

[*Laughter*].

But there's different types of Christians, right? If you are one of the Christians who believes that we can create paradise on

earth, fair fucking play to you. Fair play.
If you are one of the Christians who thinks
we can actually create fucking equality and
fellowship and joy and fucking love on this
planet, fair play, I don't want to offend
your faith in any way, faith or form … But
I am the devil, you must fist fuck me till
I bleed.

[*Laughter*]

But anyway the point being is this, I get
into quite a few rows with Christians and
especially the pro-lifers, they are the ones
that I always get in … or the anti-abortion
scum, to give them their proper name.

[*Laughter*]

They pop up every now and again and go,
'Abortion is morally wrong.' No, your very
existence disproves your point, now fuck
off …

[*Applause*]

And they're fucking incredible because they
have this whole shit of, like, we are here
to save lives. Now the year before abortion
was legalized, 250 women died at the hands
of back street abortionists, so technically
speaking you are not actually saving
fucking lives. If you wanted to save lives,
don't demonstrate outside abortion clinics,
go and fucking demonstrate somewhere where
they need people to save fucking lives. Get
outside Aeroflot offices. [*Laughter*] Big
fucking signs, 'We want planes that stay in
the air.' [*Laughter*] And, you know, I have

this big sort of argument with them as well, about, well, once the sperm reaches the egg that is human life.

This is bullshit. If you take this argument that all the life-giving fluids are sacred from God, are God given, I've got a few questions …

[*Laughter*]

If the sperm stuff, let's not be coy, if this sperm, the fucking spunk, if the *spunk* … [*Laughter*] is God given, I've got some questions and the questions basically are, if it's a God-given life form, does it get to heaven?

[*Laughter*]

Does it have angelic jizz. [*Laughter*] Wafting around, little head and a tail with wings. [*Laughter*] Because there must be fucking masses of it up there … It must be like midges in summer. [*Laughter*] Jesus … Always after *Baywatch* there's an influx. There's a right pea-souper, no that's sperm stuff. That must be just fucking incredible as it gets up there. There must masses of the stuff there because when I was 13 I ejaculated my own body weight three times.

[*Laughter*]

And if it doesn't go to heaven, does it go to hell? Because they must be fucking frying tonight, whitebait. [*Laughter*] Some of you are going. [*Sings line of 'Kum Ba Yah'*] You see the pro-lifers will always use the Bible

to back up their position. They will always
say, 'God said, "Go forth and multiply,"
therefore God loves children.' Ah. But God
also sanctioned the death of his only son,
so he doesn't like them that much.

[*Laughter*]

In my book that would put him somewhere
between the child catcher in *Chitty Chitty
Bang Bang* and Myra Hindley, just in-between
somewhere. [*Laughter*] And anyway you can
fucking prove any argument you like with
the Bible, you can prove any point of view
you like with the Bible. It's a bit like
the Scott report, any fucking point of view
is there. [*Laughter*] I can prove to you
that God wants you to take drugs, because
God sanctions it. Genesis chapter one,
verse seven. God gave us the plants and the
seeds thereof for our use. Its in the book.
Doesn't say God gave us the plants and the
seeds thereof for our partial use.

For our use …

Read between the lines. It's Jesus. No fixed
abode, moved around the countryside all his
life. [*Laughter*] With him all the time 12,
13 big burly geezers; got to be a dealer …

Got to be, got to be.

[*Laughter and applause*].

The donkey is a Jerusalem equivalent of a
BMW, sitting there like this, [*Laughter*]
sitting there like this, giving it large …
tinted blinkers. [*Laughs*]

And there was this great thing that fucking happened in London the other week. Brilliant thing on Hampstead Heath, a load of hippies and Green Party people and assorted weirdos. It was like Bertie Basset's assorted green, weird bastards, got together and they filled all these bio-degradable balloons with helium and 200 cannabis seeds and released them into London. That means the balloons float around with 200 cannabis seeds, land and biodegrade. The seeds will scatter randomly around London. There are 80 balloons, that's a fucking lot of cannabis seeds floating above London, like a fucking doped Doodle Bug, ready to drop.

[*Laughter*]

It's fucking great, all these hippies in South London going, [*Makes sucking noise*] 'Come to me.' It's fucking great because these balloons are going to land on old dears fucking council flat window boxes. [*Makes expressive noise*] And the police are, like, 'Now, what's that love?' 'Oh, I don't know?' [*Laughter*] 'Oh, you fucking do, that's a dope plant, come with me.' 'No, wait, a balloon landed and …' [*Laughter*] 'Come on love, let's just fucking go.'

But I like that. There's a campaign going at the moment. Birdseed. If you get industrial birdseed it's got fucking cannabis seed in it. It's true, the THC level is fairly low, but it's got cannabis seed in it. So sprinkle it around. Get some, sprinkle it in public places. Outside police stations would be good. [*Laughter*] Fucking great. Outside every fucking court in the country there is always one of those circular fucking concrete tubs with some shrubs in it.

That would be really cool because some bastard is going to be led in there at some point for a drug charge. They go, 'Come with me.'

'What about them?'

'Oh, fuck off, just get in.'

[*Laughter*]

It also explains why the fuck budgies spend most of the day going [*Makes noise*] I really like that mirror [*laughs*]. Fuck I could do with some cuttle, I really need cuttle big time. Also I don't know if you know, that hemp is an amazing resource. It's a great fucking eco thing, you can make clothes out of hemp, which is true. I think Marks and Spencer should bring out a fucking range. [*Laughter*] Every Christmas, [*Makes noise*] 'Oh, thanks Gran. It's a size too big, but it don't matter, I'll keep it.'

[*Laughter*]

People going to Glastonbury fully clothed, coming back naked. 'I smoked my coat.'

[*Laughter and applause*]

'Arms and Asylum'

Brighton Centre (2001),
Laughing Stock LAFFCD 0136

THOMAS

I see an incredible link between — it's not incredible, it's fucking obvious — between arms sales that we make as a country, and asylum seekers and refugees.

And this book here is, this is the *Strategic Export Control Annual Report 1999*, this lists all the arms we sold across the world in that year.

I know many of you are thinking … er, knob gag please, Mark …

[*Laughter*]

Trust me. This is fucking … It's incredible stuff 'cos you look through this and it's got … Like it lists them country by country, and how much we've sold them, and all the different types of weapons … And I was looking through this the other day because I am that sad, and I found out we sold India *anti-gravity* suits.

[*Laughter*]

We shall fight to keep Kashmir. How? We shall fly above them. [*Thumping sound*]

[*Laughter*]

281

Fucking mad. India. We sold them all these arms and, and, they come in the top 15 of countries of origin for asylum seekers.

Turkey. Here we go. This is how much we sold to Turkey in 1999. Can you just have a look? [*Shows book to audience*] 188 million quid worth of stuff. Can you see that? *188 million quid worth of arms*. And we got 4,000 refugees back the following year. So they used it, we get 4,000 people back. And you look through this stuff, it's fucking amazing, the stuff we've sold them — submachine guns, you've got body armour, and a *turret*, just the one.

[*Laughter*]

'No, we're not sure about this on the tank. No, no, we don't like the … We like open top tanks, don't we?' [*Laughter*] Sports tank.

[*Laughter*]

What else have we got here? Oh, fucking brilliant. Improvised explosive device. You see, we want you to detonate in the cinema genre, film noir. Helmet. One helmet! We've got semi-automatic pistols, laser warning detectors, we've got deactivated machine guns, deactivated projectile launchers, deactivated … This … 'We bought all this deactivated stuff. How are we going to use it?' Click.

[*Laughter*]

This is my favourite one. This is my
favourite … *General purpose machine guns.*

[*Laughter and applause*]

I thought they were fairly specific.
[*Laughter*]

'No, general purpose, you can wear it as
eveningwear.' [*Laughter*] You can kill
people with it. It says 'I'm casual, I'm
deadly.' [*Audience laughter*]

So we sold them the stuff. We get 4,000
people in return, mainly Kurds, and
tonight's show is, is basically about the
Kurds. The Kurds are the biggest single
ethnic group in the world without a
homeland or an autonomous region.
Officially there are 24 million Kurds in
the world, unofficially the Kurds say it's
40 million. If you stick with the 24
million it breaks down like this.

AUDIENCE MEMBER

40 million

THOMAS

40 million. We're going to go with 24 'cos
I don't know the figures for, for, for 40.
But if you go on that you can do your own
homework. You're students, you can do it.

[*Audience laughter*]

If you break it up, and say 12 million in
Turkey, 7 million in Iran, 4 million in
Iraq, 1 million in Syria, quarter of a
million in Azerbaijan and Armenia …

And, incredibly, the Kurds kind of came
into, sort of, Western consciousness with
Halabja in 1988, the gassing of the Kurds
by Saddam Hussein, and what happened was
not much. They really sort of came up again
in 1991, Saddam Hussein, the Gulf War … and
after the Gulf War, America said, 'We're
going to protect the Kurds in northern
Iraq. We're going to create the no-fly
zones.' They said, 'We're going to protect
you,' which is fucking worrying.

[*Laughter*]

When America says, 'We're going to protect
you,' you know you're in a prison cell and
someone's just said, 'You're going to be my
wife.'

[*Laughter*]

'Come, taste the salty champagne daddy has
prepared for you.'

[*Laughter*]

If this is the edge of liberal consensus in
Brighton, we're in for a fucking long night.

[*Laughter*]

Then, there's a whole lot of fundraising
in, and consciousness-raising done for the
Kurds in 1991.

There's benefit singles, there's benefits
organized … And the person who conceived,
ran and organized this whole thing was
Jeffrey Archer.

[*Laughter*]

When your mates are the US military and
Jeffrey Archer, you are FUCKED. [*Laughter*].
Jeffrey Archer wandering around northern
Iraq, 'Hello, marvellous to meet you, very
nice, lovely Kurds, brilliant, if anyone
asks, we're having dinner. Thursday. Dinner
night. Off we go. So …' [*Audience
laughter*]. Quick impersonation. Ah, stop
it, it hurts. That's Jeffrey in about half
an hour's time with any luck.

[*Laughter*]

So … The incredible thing was, and it's
about six years ago, evidence … I want to
say evidence.

They're not fucking just bits of paper,
these are video fucking evidence of the
butchery and that, that even doesn't convey
what happened, the *butchery* that went on
when the Turkish authorities came over,
entered the border, entered northern Iraq
and started murdering Kurds.

And you think, hang on a minute, because I
thought we're protecting them. Then this
year American service personnel say, 'We've
been told to keep our planes on the ground,
turn off the radar and monitoring equipment
and when we fly over the areas we're
supposed to be protecting, we find the
Turkish authorities have bombed fuck out of
it.'

You go, well, I spoke to … I thought we
were looking after these people. Who is a
good Kurd, who are the bad Kurds?

According to the West, who are the good Kurds, who are the bad Kurds? I think I've sussed it. Bear with me. It works like this. Northern Iraqi Kurds are lovely Kurds. You're tip-top Kurds because you hate Saddam and we hate Saddam, therefore we love you. Turkish Kurds, boo Kurd, bad Kurd, hiss Kurd, get in the box Kurd because Turkey we love 'cos they're in NATO, lots of contracts, they hate you, therefore you're shit. Meanwhile, if Turkey attacks the northern Iraqi Kurds, you're shit as well. If Saddam attacks you, you're lovely. It depends on who's beating the fuck out of you is whether you're good or you're bad. Syria, it depends on who's in ascendancy, Socialists or Democrats. We don't know. Meanwhile, in Iran, fucking hell, we fucking love the Iranian Kurds because they hate Iran and we hate Iran except they hate Iran from fucking Iraq.

[*Audience laughter*]

Bad Kurd. So, Azerbaijan, I mean, for a quarter of a million we don't give a shit. So, basically the person who works out who's a good Kurd and who's a bad Kurd according to the West is the same person who devises the timetable for Railtrack. That's roughly, [*Laughter, applause*] how it works …

[*Applause*]

'The War on Terror'

Edinburgh (2004),
Laughing Stock LAFFCD 0166

THOMAS

You see this is why Bush has got to have this war in Iraq, because he said, I'm going to wage war on terror, which is a mistake, because terror is a concept.

[*Laughter*]

How can you wage a war on a concept? An abstract? Fine, you want war on abstract concepts? Fucking great, you kill a lot less people.

[*Laughter*]

Good, let's have a war on clutter next. Fucking bring 'em on.

[*Laughter*]

You can't bomb a concept, George. Do, do, dah, okay.

[*Laughter*]

Sorry, and it's hard, how do you fucking fight al-Qaeda, anyway? How do you wage a war, like a traditional war, you know, like your proper fucking war, you know, your proper war, where fucking thousands of yer working classes are senselessly slaughtered to bring down the unemployment figures? How can you fucking have a proper war?

287

[*Laughter*]

I thought you'd have fucking known that all
up here, wouldn't you?

[*Laughter*]

Fucking British ruling class fucking hate
the jocks until there's a fucking war on,
then they love you.

[*Laughter*]

It's just incredible that is, it's just
fucking incredible, because how can you
have a war on al-Qaeda? They're an
international terror group that work
fucking transnational. They are linked
through a series of video releases by their
messianic beardy, wispy one, that kind of
Islamic fundamentalist dashed in with a bit
of anti-imperialism sliced in with a little
bit of fucking anti-consumerism, anti-
commercialism, with a little bit of a wispy
cat weasel beard as well … beep

[*Laughter*]

And he is off. There's no sort of standing
hierarchy or structure. There's no fucking
attack network. How the fuck do you bomb
that? It's like, you know, like a game of
battleships.

[*Laughter*]

B3.

[*Laughter*]

Miss.

[*Laughter*]

Ooh no, you got my Chinese embassy. Did you mean to do that?

[*Laughter and applause*].

Bush, man, did you see the fucking one o'clock broadcast the other night? 'Saddam Hussein has got 48 hours.' What do, what do you think he was going to do? Saddam Hussein, 'Quick, bring my sons and the travel catalogues.'

[*Laughter*]

What the fuck is he going to do? I tell you a great thing to do, because the propaganda's coming out well and fucking truly now, it's really fucking pouring out of those screens. This is my best way of, I've come up with of countering the propaganda. Right, when you see Bush or Blair appear on the television screen, just start humming to yourself, bah-bah-bah-bah-bah-bah.

[*Laughter*]

And when you see us lot, go, biddy, dee-dee.

[*Laughter*]

It's just fucking incredible, because Bush has wanted a war for ages. He's been driving the bus to war town. He's been driving the bus. He's at the wheel. He's got a big fucking yellow school bus. On the bus is every fucking country in the world,

289

and he's there going, 'You've got to get
Saddam Hussein, you've got to get Saddam
Hussein, hm. Got to get Saddam, because he
could have nuclear weapons. North Korea
shut the fuck up.'

[*Laughter*]

'Got to get Saddam Hussein. India,
Pakistan, I can reach you from up here, you
know. We've got to get Saddam Hussein,
because Saddam Hussein gassed his own
people. Russia, stop playing with the
windows.'

[*Laughter*]

'We've got to get Saddam Hussein. Saddam
Hussein invaded Kuwait; he invaded another
country. Israel, are you sitting in
Palestine's seat?'

[*Laughter*]

'Are you Israel?'

[*Laughter and applause*]

'Israel you'd better be sitting in
Palestine's seat, because I paid for you
to.'

[*Laughter*]

And I know you re thinking, Mark, but where
is Tony Blair on this bus? He isn't on the
bus; he's on the bonnet, right in the
front.

[*Laughter*]

He is the fucking point man for barbarity and murder. That fucking man is an evil pig dog. He opens his mouth and fucking words come out like Milli Vanilli never fucking went away.

[*Laughter and applause*].

Yes, Mark, but what do you think the peace movement has achieved? We put ten years on that fucker, and that's enough.

[*Laughter*]

Ten years. Somewhere in Downing Street there's a portrait getting younger, and that fucking suits me just fine.

[*Laughter*]

What I want to see now are adverts on the television, with some bloke sitting in a chair going, 'I could pull a dead body out the water, I could tell someone that their child had died. But be Clare Short, no I couldn't do that.'

[*Laughter and applause*].

You know the amazing this is you look at the excuses that they've rolled out. The excuses. I mean God bless the Labour rebels. The fuck, I don't know what, how was the breakdown of the 217? I don't know how many were Labour. Anyone know?

AUDIENCE

132.

THOMAS

132 rebels? Where did they get the spines
from? Why, it's incredible, [*Laughing*] I
don't know where they found them, but they
did. Because normally they say, 'We're
going to have a backbench rebellion Mark.'
'Oh, really?' 'Yes.' 'Oh?'

[*Laughter*]

That'll, oh, that will be very exciting.
Yeah, it is. Is Tony frightened? Yeah.

[*Laughter*]

Yeah, no, is it seriously. Oh, is it
really? 'We're having a vote on why we're
not allowed to have a vote, and some of us
might abstain …'

[*Laughter*]

So the amazing thing is the excuses they
come up with for this war. You start, cast
your mind back, because you did have all
that, 'Gotta get Saddam Hussein, gotta get
Saddam because he was a terrorist. He was
not democratically elected.'

[*Laughter*]

There are other reasons. 'Got to get Saddam
Hussein because his weapons of mass
destruction, he has told us what he's got.
He has told us some of the things he's got.
We've destroyed some of the things he's
got, but we don't know what he's got left
hiding there.'

Well get your old copy of the invoice and flick through …

[*Laughter*]

So you look at the excuses, and you go back to about six weeks ago. 'That Saddam Hussein, we have found evidence of his weapons of mass destruction.' 11 shell cases. 11. 11.

I can take you to pubs down the fucking road …

[*Laughter*]

11 shell cases, which then turned out, the shell cases turned out to be 12 years old, which in sort of military terms is fucking ancient. It's like a Hans Blick had the fucking Time Team in there with it.

[*Laughter*]

And so Tony Robinson was wandering around, looking for Saddam's muskets of mass destruction.

[*Laughter*]

All those fucking trenches. They say, look, he's building trenches round. No, it's they're building, they're looking for fucking remains, and those twats wandering around … 'I don't do much, but I got a funny hat.'

[*Laughter*]

Then Bush says, 'We have evidence that Saddam Hussein is linked to al-Qaeda.'

Will you show us now?

[*Laughter*]

No, he doesn't want to, like, it's not a fucking game of Happy Families. 'Have you got Mr Bin Laden the Bomber?'

[*Laughter*]

Then there's Co-lin Powell, whose name is Colin …

[*Laughter and applause*].

You can have 'Colin' or 'Colon', you can't have fucking 'Co-lin'. If it's 'Co-lin', his surname is pronounced 'Poo-weel'.

[*Laughter*]

His boss is called 'G-orgy Boosh'.

[*Laughter*]

And Rumsfeld is pronounced 'Cunt'.

[*Laughter and applause*].

So there's fucking Co-lin, Colin, whatever, evidence of Saddam's weapons of mass destruction. It's grainy photograph number one. [*Puffs*] 'See here, satellite photograph of an Iraqi installation. Note forklift truck.'

[*Laughter*]

'Grainy photo number two. [*Puffs*] Same installation, three months later. Forklift truck has moved.'

[*Laughter*]

Speaks for itself. 'Now we have transcripts of telephone calls from random Iraqis.' This is the translation. 'Hoo-ha-ha, ha-ha, we have thwarted the evil pig dogs from America. Hoo-ha-ha, ha-ha.'

[*Laughter*]

That's not fucking evidence. There are British courts that wouldn't convict on that fucking evidence, not in the seventies, and not with an Irish defendant.

[*Laughter and applause*].

Evidence. Fucking even David Icke was going, 'it's a bit of a shaky theory, isn't it?'

[*Laughter*]

Then it turns out British Intelligence have fucking nicked their report from a student, like obviously they didn't literally nick it, because otherwise the student would be going into class, going, 'Me dissertation …'

[*Laughter*]

'Erm … James Bond'.

[*Laughter*]

And Bush and all of that lot are useless … I think Bush is actually getting his excuses from Ron Davis.

[*Laughter*]

Oh dear. 'We're not invading Iraq; we're looking for badgers.'

[*Some audience members hiss*]

What do you mean, [*Gasp*] ooh, [*Gasp*] ooh? That was crazy, [*Laughing*] that was so Edinburgh. God bless you.

[*Laughter*]

[*Gasp*] Ooh, [*Gasp*] ooh, no man, you could get away with that on the West Coast, but not here.

[*Laughter and applause*].

Ron Davis would have been fucking fired if he'd just, 'fessed up you know, 'I do like to suck a bit of an old man's cock anyway.'

[*Laughter*]

Looking for badger! He could have said, you know, 'I do, I just like a, you know, a taste of an old man's tonkey, you know.'

[*Laughter*]

'You know, fucking fair play to me, at least I'm not fucking Edwina Currie and John Major.'

[*Laughter*]

And then we'd have all forgiven him, because that's a horrible image.

[*Laughter*]

There's Edwina …

[*Laughter*] Aah.

[*Laughter*] And she's got one like that.

And if we have any more of those hisses and gasps you get the whole fucking description.

[*Laughter*]

So. The fucking thing that gets me though is all this bollocks that you get in the press, because if you're against the war, and against the bombing of civilians, then, 'Oh, you're nothing but an apologist for Saddam Hussein.' And it's quite playgroundy, because it's, 'Saddam is your boyfriend. Chi-chi-chi-chi.'

[*Laughter*]

And it's just like that. The fucking *Mail* is fucking the worst. Do you know; a tree died for that shit?

[*Laughter*]

And you just sort of think, you know, I, I am against the bombing. Ah, you bastard, lesbian, asylum-seeking, fucking Algerian. They have big racing strapping dildos and they want to bugger us in front of our children.

[*Laughter*]

And that's a quote.

[*Laughter*]

I do support our troops. Our troops should be supported. They should fucking come home and be where they should be, away from murder, away from murdering, playing table

football. That's what they should be
fucking doing.

[*Laughter*]

That's where they should be.

[*Applause*].

Or, vaulting over horses, live in the *Blue
Peter* studio.

[*Laughter*]

I want to go out there and go, 'Come on,
wouldn't you rather be back at barracks,
painting each other bollocks black with
shoe polish?' 'Come on …'

LAUGHING STOCK PRODUCTIONS

Laughing Stock Productions was formed by three friends in 1992 to fill the gap between the audio comedy that was available from the BBC, which was mainly archive radio shows, and the scant number of American imports and one-off releases from British record companies.

The idea was to start a record label that would re-issue deleted British records, and also originate recordings by new and established stand up comedians. We knew that 'back in the sixties' comedy records were big business (even I remember as a child sitting around with the whole family listening to Barry Humphries, Bill Cosby and Shelly Berman records), so the business plan was somehow to re-establish a boom in comedy record sales, make millions, and then retire to opulent comedy mansions in the country.

Sadly, the various banks we approached didn't share this optimism, and so it was left to Colin Collino, a disillusioned doctor of medicine who also owned a cassette-manufacturing business, to fund the launch of the business. Comedy agent Pete Brown, who had formed Talkback with Mel & Griff, was the comedy contacts man. My role was to scour record company archives for deleted comedy gems and to bring my somewhat limited 'business affairs' experience to the task of signing and licensing material to the label.

Within six months, we had secured rights to, and were manufacturing cassettes (!) by Rowan Atkinson, Billy Connolly, Ben Elton and Bill Hicks. We were also re-issuing *The World of Pete & Dud* and Amnesty International's *The Secret Policeman's Ball*, plus some vintage Groucho Marx and Bill Cosby live recordings. Our first original recording was of

Scottish comedian Arnold Brown, a Perrier Award winner and one of the original Comic Strip crew, which was recorded at the 1991 Edinburgh Festival.

Tragically, Pete Brown died suddenly of a brain haemorrhage in 1993. Not only had Colin and I lost a great friend, but now the future of the company was in doubt, as Pete had been our main contact with the people who mattered in the comedy industry. However, thanks to the kindness and trust shown to us by Vivienne Clore, Caroline Chignell and Bruce Hills (Richard Stone Partnership, PBJ Management and Just for Laughs respectively), we were able to carry on and released recordings by artists such as Eddie Izzard, Jo Brand, Rory Bremner, Greg Proops, Bird & Fortune, Sean Hughes, Mark Thomas, and lots of American comedy.

In 1998, we released the *Very Best of Laughing Stock*, a collection of our favourite and bestselling artists, a copy of which is attached this book.

Of all entertainment, I think stand-up comedy is the most exciting. Combining the painstaking thought that goes into a comic's act, the energy and immediacy of a live gig, and the ability of one person to silence a basement full of drunks, or to hold the attention of a packed out concert hall, with something as pure and simple as a *joke*, stand-up is a feat that never ceases to delight.

Mike O'Brien

CD TRACK LIST

1. Rowan Atkinson & MONTY PYTHON
   'THE FOUR YORKSHIREMEN'
   ℗ Amnesty International

2. Jo Brand
   'HASTINGS'
   ℗ Laughing Stock Productions

3. Rory Bremner
   'JOHN MAJOR / THE QUEEN'
   ℗ Laughing Stock Productions

4. Arnold Brown
   'The Secret of Comedy'
   ℗ Laughing Stock Productions

5. Steve Coogan
   'Paul Calf'
   ℗ Terrence Higgins Trust

6. Pete & Dud
   'The Psychiatrist'
   ℗ Tro Essex Music

7. Lenny Henry
   'Delbert Wilkins'
   ℗ Amnesty International

8. Bill Hicks
    'What Is Pornography?' from *Relentless*
    Invasion Group Ltd. © 1997 Rykodisc

9. Sean Hughes
    'NIGHTCLUBS'
    ℗Laughing Stock Productions

10. Eddie Izzard
    'CATS & DOGS'
    ℗Ella Communications

11. Greg Proops
    'PILGIMS & PSYCHOCHRISTIANS'
    ℗Laughing Stock Productions

12. Monty Python
    'The Parrot Sketch'
    ℗Amnesty International

13. Mark Thomas
    'The War on Terror'
    ℗Laughing Stock Productions